BOOK OF MICHAEL A SON OF GOD AND BROTHER OF OUR LORD JESUS CHRIST

DON STEWART

For Greg and Valerie
Thanks for everything
Bless you guys
In our Lord

Michael
Darling

To my understanding of scripture thus far. I've pondered on this verse to understand it and its entirety. I've come to understand it in this way. 1) scripture says "and they will call Him Immanuel" meaning God with us. 2) it also says that He is in the Father and the Father is in Him. 3) Also, Jesus is the Son of God (the Father) so He carries the Fathers name. As Jesus said, "before Abraham was, I AM. 4) God said to Moses " and you shall be like God to Aaron and Aaron shall be like God to the people. 5) and again, Jesus quoted the old testament when He said, "I have made you Gods" 6) Jesus also confirmed this when one of the disciples came to Him and said, " Lord your mother and brother are looking for you". Jesus replied with, " Who are my mothers and brothers? Truly truly I say unto you, here are my mothers and brothers, those who do the will of My Father in Heaven are my mothers and brothers and sisters". 7) so, if we are Jesus' brothers and we are indeed our Fathers children then are we not gods? Though we are not the Almighty God, but we are His children. 8) Also, scripture states that God the Father is in the Son and the Son is in the Father and that The Son is in us (the sons) and we are in Him. Which also means the Father is in us (the sons) and we (the sons) are in the Father. And if this is true then He is God the Father and we would indeed be His godly children. 9) our Father also gives us Godly gifts to His godly children, like healing, prophecy, speaking in tongs, walking on water (Peter did it), faith and so much more. 10) scripture also says that if we are His children and that the earth and all that is in it is His and that we are heirs and that everything created is also ours. 11) One True God our Father and one True Godly Son namely Jesus. many godly children (us). 12) so, Jesus is like God to us, for it is only through Him can we come to the Father. Amen

I Am that I Am, I Am a Son of God The Everlasting Father, and Brother of His Beloved Son Jesus. Born again- spiritual age? Other brothers and I are sent out to the fields and wilderness to find our lost brothers and lead them home. To give directions to our brothers looking for the way home, and for those on the way but still need more directions. To lead them home to The Son (our oldest Brother), who is the way to the Father.

Special   Thanks

I give thanks first to our Heavenly Father, for putting it in my heart to wright this and for His great love, mercy and grace for allowing me to wright this. I thank my family for being patient with me for my time spent on this project. I thank those who have helped me in this project. I thank my wife April Stewart and my daughter Elizabeth Gregory for helping me transfer this book from hand written to digital format and for showing me how to get started using Microsoft Word. And a thank you to my nephew Marcus Stewart for the cover photo.

Cover photo is taken and used in memory of my mother. Thanks mom for planting the seed of our Lord in me at an early age. Love and miss you..

Author/ Writer Brad Stevens for helping with Editing.

By: Author/ Writer, Don (Michael) Stewart JR.

dedication

This book is dedicated to you, the reader, to all my brothers and sisters and potential brothers and sisters. And I pray that these writings will help you in your walk with one another, our Lord Jesus and our Heavenly Father. May our Father bless us all in doing His work and living in His will.

Introduction

This book is designed and written to help us all as His children to understand what it means to be a child of God and how He expects us to walk in our daily lives and how we should love one another.

•

CONTENTS

1) WE ARE FAMILY

2) GOD'S LOVE

3) READING SCRIPTURE

4) PRAYER

5) MARRIAGE

6) DIFFERENT BIBLE TRANSLATIONS

7) CHRISTIANS AND WORLDLY CHRISTIANS

8) CHRIST AND THE DIFFERENT DENOMINATIONS

WE ARE FAMILY

My blessed brothers and sisters, I am writing you because I believe our Father has put it on my heart to do so. This is a call to action for all of those who are children of the Living Father (The Only True Living God). Brothers and sisters, it is time we wake up and start truly living the life our Father has called us to live: In the ways of our Father and no longer in the ways of the world.

2) Like adopted children, when they have been accepted into their new family also inherit the family name. This results in, not only a change of name but also a changed life which forever alters the child at the core of who they are. As the child spends more time with the family, their bond grows. Soon the child starts to feel and believe they are a true part of the family, especially as they experience love for one another. As they were once strangers to each other, now they are family. And it all started with a parent who loved a lost child enough to adopt them and bring them into their home as one of their own. The more quality time they spend together the stronger the relationship grows. Through the good times and the bad, they continue to grow as a natural family while at the same time learning to love each. The natural born children grow together with the adopted children and over time, by the grace of God, they develop a strong love for one another.

3) Although humanity is God's creation, because of the rebellion of mankind against our creator, our relationship is strained. God has not turned His back on us so much as we have turned our back on Him. If we return to Him and humble ourselves before Him by grace through faith in the work of Jesus, then we are adopted into His family. We once again become His children. We have been joined to a new family. In a sense, we are reborn into a new family. Not just any family but a Holy Family. The Holy Family of God, who is now our Father, your Father.

4) What normally happens to a person's name when they enter into a new family by birth or adoption? They are given a new family name. In scripture many times God the Father changes a person's name, after they recognize Him for who He is and start walking in His ways. It is the same way with us today. Just as we carry our earthly father's name, we also carry our Heavenly Father's name. Our earthly father's name comes last but our Heavenly Father's name comes first. Most of us say it without realizing it. Every time we introduce ourselves, we say it.

5) Before I reveal this mystery let's look at God's name according to scripture. Sure there are many names for God but there are two particular names we need to look at. The first is in Genesis starting with the man Abram, whose name was later changed by God to Abraham. In Hebrew, Abraham called God YHWH (YAHEW), in Greek or old English it's translated to Yehovah and in new English Jehovah. Either way the true meaning is I AM THAT I AM. In Exodus Moses ask God His name, God told him, I AM THAT I AM. As it is with us. If we used biblical terms my name would be like, I AM Michael son of Don from the tribe of Stewart (Michael son of God). Or in today's terms, I AM Don Michael Stewart (God's son Michael) See that? Our Heavenly Father's name first, earthly father's name comes last.

6) There's a lot to be said about a person's name. This too is found all through the scriptures. Usually the life of one was lived by the meaning of their name. My name, for example is Don Michael. Growing up I was always called Michael. At an early age of going to church, I learned the meaning of the name Michael. Not only did I learn that it was the name of God's arch angel (which was cool) but the meaning was even cooler: to be like God.

7) But I didn't really like the name Don. Primarily because of some of its meanings Such as the name for a mafia boss or something like that, at least I didn't until recently. Months ago, I was reading a book, studying scripture, and the author was writing about wearing your

armor. Your spiritual armor, the armor of God. He noted how we must grow into our armor to grow into God - to grow into who the Father wants us to be. He talked about David getting ready to fight Goliath. Before he went to battle, King Saul offered David his armor. The armor did not fit David. He would need time to test it and grow into it. The reason for that was because it wasn't David's armor, it was made for Saul.

8) Each of us have a spiritual armor made by God, our Father. You start by putting it on and wearing it. After that you're going to have to test it and grow into it. If you're not ready to wear it, you need to be trained. You need training to grow and be all your Father has planned for you. It's like a parent, who buys clothing for their children a couple sizes too big, so the child can grow into the clothing. The same is true about your spiritual armor and your relationship with your Father.

9) In the book that I was studying I saw the words "don your mantel" which piqued my interest. So, I looked it up and found that in Hebrew, Don means to grow into, to conform and to wear with might. And Stewart means to be a keeper of the house. In essence then, my name means to grow to learn to be like God to be a keeper of the house. Pretty cool name, I thought.

10) My prayer is that I can and will live out the meaning of my name. "I AM Don Michael Stewart". I am to continually grow to be like my God, my Father, to be a keeper of the house, Amen. For all these years I've been called Michael, does this mean that my name has been "changed" to Don Michael? Perhaps. More people have called me Don these last couple years than ever before.

11) What is the meaning of your name? Is there a Hebrew meaning to your name? I've heard people ask, "What is your Christian name?" This has puzzled me for some time. I was aware that a lot of people chosen by God were given a different name after receiving their calling from Him. Some examples from the Bible such as

Abram/Abraham, Jacob/Israel, and Saul/Paul, to name a few. For instance, Peter, the one most widely known for denying Christ three times, also received a name change. His birth name was Simon, meaning "hear and listen". When Jesus called out to Simon, "Come follow me and I will make you fishers of men". Simon, like his name, heard and listened. As it is written, "my sheep know the sound of my voice". Shortly after following Jesus, our Lord changed Simon's name to Peter, meaning Rock. Towards the end of Jesus ministry, Jesus said to Peter in Matthew 16:18 "And I tell you, you are Peter, and on this Rock I will build my church". And upon that rock, He did, and continues to build His church. Peter's name described what kind of life he was going to live, according to the name given him.

12) David's name, on the other hand, means "beloved". David is the son of Jesse. Jesse means God exist or God's gift. As if to say, Jesse means God's gift to His people through Jesse and through David (a king), comes the birth of Jesus (The One True King).

13) About the time David defeated Goliath, David was in his late teens and worked as a shepherd, similar to our Lord Jesus who is a Shepherd to us, His sheep. David was also a musician, who played the harp, often playing for God. David not only played an instrument, but also wrote songs and poems about, to, and for, God. During this time God said in 1 Samuel 13:14 "I have found David, son of Jesse, a man after my own heart". After Saul's death God would remove kingship from Saul's house to David's. Although David would be anointed kingship years before. That is why Saul sought to kill David.

14) Like a loving Father, who also disciplines His children, David on several occasions received punishment when he messed up or sinned against God. After one act of sin, God gave David a choice. He offered David three different kinds of punishment and told David to pick one. Each time we receive a punishment, it's a way of our Father saying, my child you're starting to go the wrong direction. That way

leads to destruction. The ways of this world lead to destruction. The punishments here on Earth is a way of our Father giving us a taste of what we'll receive if we keep going down the wrong path.

15) For example, you can tell your children all day long that the stovetop is hot, don't touch it. It will burn you. But unfortunately, we are sinful and have free will, so we just have to touch the hot stovetop to see for ourselves....Ouch!! Now we know why we shouldn't touch the stove. Will we put our hands back on that hot stovetop again? Probably not on purpose. As the saying goes: No pain, no gain. Would it have not been better to just listen to our Father the first time? Is this not the same things we try to teach our own children?

16) So, David lived by the meaning of his name throughout his life. We should ponder on what our name means and how to live according to not only the name He has given you, but His will for your life. Like God's armor that He made for you. Your name is like a tool you're going to need for your work. Take your job position, and your tools (armor of God) and go to work. You're like a soldier, going out to war. But instead of killing your enemy, your job is to save him. He may hate you but your job as a child of God is to love him, and try to snatch him from the fire, to save his soul.

17) Keep your armor on at all times. In ancient times a soldier even slept with his armor on; we too must always be ready. Always be ready to share your cup with others. Take what God has given you and hand it down to someone else. Blessings are like hand-me-downs. You receive a blessing and then you hand it down for someone else to enjoy. They, in turn, bless another. When you share your blessings with others in need, you get it back or receive another blessing. The more you give the more you get back. Your job is to look for lost sheep, bring them home, grow the Family. As you were once lost, but now are found, and have become a member of the Family. Now go and live out your name. You belong to the Father, and carry His name, I

Am. Do as He does, as His Son and His Spirit do. Follow His ways to have, show and share. His Love, Mercy, Grace and Peace.

God's Love

God's love is so deep, that we as humans, will never be able to fully understand just how great this love is. As humans, it is difficult to understand why a loving God would allow evil and bad things to happen. I read somewhere that God said that evil must take its course! For me, I believe that there is a great blessing that comes out of this. First of all, the scripture mentions many times that there is a blessing in suffering. Look at Jesus, His disciples, and many other followers. Second, if we can follow God's will, these evil acts that happen, help us grow, and makes us stronger in our faith. As it is written, "what man has intended for evil, I will use for good".

1) I believe this helps us in our growth by demonstrating true love. The bible mentions many times how God refines His children, like gold being refined (purified) by fire. Some examples are found in Psalm 12:6, Isaiah 1:25, 1 Peter 1:7, Psalm 77:10-12, Daniel 11:35, Zachariah 13:9, Malachi 3:2-3, Job 23:10, and Isaiah 48:10, just to name a few. I believe that all the bad and evil is allowed to make us stronger, more loving, more merciful, more forgiving, and more caring.

2) In Romans 12:18-21 and 1 Peter 3:9-14 talks about repaying evil with good. This is demonstrated through the grand example Jesus laid out for us. Through all of His torture, not once did He curse anyone. Neither did Steven when he was being stoned to death. Instead, as he was being stoned to death, he prayed for those who were stoning him. In James 3:10 we read, "From the same mouth comes blessings and cursing, my brothers, these things should not be done. As scripture states, love your enemies, do good to those who hate you, bless those who curse you, pray for those who mistreat you.

3) In Ezekiel 18:23, God said "Do I take pleasure in the death of the wicked? Decllareth the Lord. Of course not! I want them to turn from their wicked ways and live." To turn their heart to me and do good, and I will them and save their soul. For we are all created in His Image. This is why we should not curse our enemy but love them and pray for them. So that they too may come to the Lord. For example, in Matthew 13:24, Jesus speaks of a man who planted good seed in a field. While the workers were asleep, an enemy came and planted weeds (bad seed) in with the wheat (good seed). The workers asked their master, "Lord shall we go and remove the weeds?". The Master said, "No, lest you pull up the wheat also. Let them grow together, then at the harvest, separate the weeds from the wheat and throw the weeds into the fire. But store the wheat in my barn".

4) As a lawn guy, I've learned that to keep a healthy lawn is to keep it maintained well. One process is to apply a weed-n-feed twice a year. In doing this repeatedly it causes the grass to grow healthier while at the same time, the weeds start to get choked out. Over time the weeds will start to disappear. After a little time, a little work, and time invested you will soon have a nice-looking yard. Our life is much the same, we keep the weeds out of our lives by focusing our eyes and ears on God's love us and for all his children, while continually feeding on God's word. The Bible can be used like a weed-n-feed. Scripture is food for our soul. It also teaches us how to fight against sin in our lives (how to get rid of the weeds in our yard).

5) It's important not to neglect your yard. If we keep ourselves fed, and feed others with God's word, will, and love then we will grow healthy and choke out evil. But when we neglect God's word, will, and love, we are then neglecting our yard, and evil closes in all around us, like a yard filled with weeds that chokes out the grass. Your yard is the people around you. Keep it fed by showing them God's love, so that by working together, and loving everyone and showing God's love to

everyone we may choke out the evil weeds and start producing a beautiful yard, a beautiful field, and beautiful children of the Father.

6) God has many loves. Most of us have heard about the word love and how it's used in Hebrew. Most of us have learned that in Hebrew, the use of love as in the love of a parent is one word, the love of a sibling another, the love of a friend, the love of a spouse, the love of mercy and encouragement are all different types of love. In Hebrew, there was one word that brings all of these different meanings into one word, "Dodekha" which means loves, as in, a plural word for God's many different kinds of loves, all rolled up into one word. A Dodekha love, that's the love of a friend, brother, love of a husband, father, love of encouragement and mercy. And no matter how loving you think the Father is, He is ever more loving.

7) Scripture says "God is love" and since we are called as children of God, we are to be like God. To be like God is to be love. Be love. And love covers many sins. To be a child of God is to love all. How many of us would put our only son on a cross to die for the sins of billions of people? No mind can possibly imagine the amount of sin that occurs in one day, all around the world, and these sins have continued every day for thousands of years. Would you give up your son who was righteous and loving in every way so that a murderer could live?

8) It's sad to know that most people will not accept this love. It is in fact a great love. For those of us who have accepted Christ, that love is within our reach. For those of us who believe and belong to the Family, are called to receive this love and to share this love with all of those around us, so that we can see it grow all around us.

9) Like a good shepherd, who feeds his flock, God the Father sent His Son to Earth, the field, to spread his version of weed-n-feed, love. To feed his flock, to feed his people. Showing us true love so that we can become a healthy yard, filled with love, caring, and nurturing. And in doing so, we choke evil out of our lives (the weeds).

10) Now instead of going to the cross, our Lord Jesus could have turned and run away. He knew His time on Earth in the flesh was drawing near to an end. He even prayed about it. In Matthew 26:39, Luke 22:42 and Mark 14:36, Jesus asked the Father to remove the cup that He was about to drink but if it was the Father's will He would drink it. He wanted to do the Father's will not His own. By the grace of God, our Lord stayed with the plan and followed His Father's will.

11) In Matthew 12:47-49, one of the disciples said to Jesus, "Lord, your mother and brother are looking for you." Jesus replied "Who is My mother and brother?" Then speaking about those who were in the room with Him, His followers, He said: "Truly, truly I say to you, here are My mothers and brothers and sisters. Those who do the will of My Father in Heaven are my mothers and brothers and sisters". Wow! How amazing that our Lord called us His brothers and sisters! We are not just siblings to one another, but siblings to our Lord. We can call Him our Big Brother, our oldest sibling. He is trying to teach us how to work in the Family business. The kind of business that profits by love, not money.

12) In 1 Timothy 5:2, 1 Corinthians 1:26, Acts 6:3, and many other places, we are told to recognize each other as brothers and sisters. If we are truly children of the Father, then we are true brothers and sisters of Christ, to His Angels and to each other. This is another reason why it's important to show love to everyone, to do good to everyone and not evil. As scripture states, especially to those who belong to the Faith, the Family. It's important to understand that since we cannot simply look around and tell who are the children of God, the Father, the only solution is to treat everyone you come across as if they are brothers or sisters but also knowing that most are not. If you do know who is not a believer, or know someone who doesn't belong to the Family, then they are potential brothers and sisters. When you show love to the lost, you are indeed shining the Light of God into their lives as well, just as God loved you when you were lost, and now you are a child of God.

13) We cannot truly see the Father's love if we are not willing to share His love, even to our enemies, to those you don't like so much, to the poor, the liar, the thief, the ones who make it hard to love them because they are just so mean and yes; even the murder. Remember David had Uriah the Hittite killed because David slept with his wife. Also Saul (Paul) killed and imprisoned people for proclaiming Jesus as Lord.

14) How many of us who are Christians have a worldly brother, sister, spouse, or even a child who doesn't believe in God? Yet, we still love them as our family. Do we not continue to try to help them in their struggle, and show them love when we're around them? How many of us are quick to curse at someone for what they have said or done? I've even heard Christians say "They should go to hell for that" or "There is a special place in hell for people like that". That is not a good thing. In fact, it's quite evil to say such things.

15) Scripture says we should not speak evil but let words of grace and blessings flow from our lips. Jesus said "It's not what goes into the mouth that makes you unclean but what comes out of your mouth". When you speak evil of or to someone, you are in fact making yourself unclean. Jesus also said, even if you go into a private place and speak evil, that to will be brought to light. Maybe we should carry a bar of soap around our neck so we can wash our filthy mouth when we speak evil against or to someone. Even if you're all alone, God still hears your words and your thoughts.

16) Remember: we are all sinners and we all deserve hell. Hell is not a good place, it is an eternal torture. This is according to Revelation 20:14, 21:8, 2:11 and 20:6. This is called the eternal lake of fire and is the second death for the wicked. It is the wrath of God that should be feared. For this is destruction of the soul. Scripture says not to fear man who can only destroy the flesh, but to fear Him who can destroy both flesh and soul. To show His love for us, our Father doesn't want to cast

us into the eternal lake of fire but rather He wants to free us from it. Our Father wants to save His children.

17) But because we are disobedient children our tendency is to keep digging ourselves into holes we can't get out of on our own. Because of our selfishness, ignorance and rebellion (yes, myself included), we owe a debt to God. The payment is called atonement and it can only be paid with blood; It will cost the blood of an innocent person laying down his life for you.

18) In the Old Testament the blood of an animal was accepted as atonement, but that didn't actually take care of the problem it only looked forward to the promise of God to provide a way of being set free. It would cost the blood of a man, but not just any man would cover the sins of the world. It would and could only be one particular man a man without sin. Out of all the billions of men who have lived, only one man in particular was qualified for this job, Jesus Christ, the Son of God the Father, our Lord, our King, our Brother. Through Him we are saved and redeemed by the Grace of our Father.

19) Our Lord and Brother Jesus said: "There is no greater love then that of one who would lay down his own life for a friend." Scripture also reflects on this. It speaks about how once we become believers, we are no longer friends but family. In scripture, we read "older women be like mothers to the younger, young women be like sisters; men be like brothers, for such you are".

20) Now if indeed sin is the enemy, it would seem fair to say that there is no greater love than that of whom would lay down his own life for an enemy. Think about that, an innocent man laying down his life so that his enemy can be saved and truly live. Wow, wow, wow! That changes everything. He died for the murderer, the liar, the thief, the rapist, the child molester, those in terrorist groups, the worst kind of people, and yes, even you and me. For God does not delight in the

death of the wicked, but that the wicked turn from their wickedness to God, to the Father, and do good.

21) As humans, we separate one crime from another. We want to judge people according to their sin, or by the law that was broken. Small sentence for a small crime, and a larger sentence for a larger crime...We don't have the understanding of God the Father. For in the eyes of the Father, a sin is a sin. A murderer is no worse than a liar. As in Revelation 21:8 they will both end up in the same place with the same sentence. Yet if any wicked man will turn from his wicked ways and come to Me and do good and walk in all My ways. Then I will heal his heart and save his soul.

22) Now once that evil man has accepted the Lord, he is now known as a child of the Father, and a brother to His children. We should, in the same way as our Father, show the same love, mercy, and forgiveness that the Father shows us. Paul wrote in Galatians 6:10 "Therefore, whenever we have the opportunity we should do good to everyone, especially to those who belong to the Family of Faith.

23) In Matthew 18:21-22, Peter asked Jesus, "How many times should I forgive my brother in one day, what seven times?" Jesus replied, "Not just seven times, but seventy times seven. As many times as he sins against you if he asks you for your forgiveness and repents each time, you must forgive him each time". He also said, we must forgive from the heart. I think it's very important, brothers and sisters, that we learn to do this out of love not because we have to but because we want to, because we love them. We want them to be saved as well. Now if you feel as if someone doesn't deserve your grace, then neither do you deserve the Father's grace. And yet the Father shows you Grace, therefore we are to be like the Father, be like the Son, be a son and daughter and show the same grace to them that the Father has shown us. What did God tell Mosses to say to the people? Least they say, its because of my righteousness that the Lord has done this. Thus its

because of grace and mercy. Again, God told Mosses," I will have mercy on whom I choose to have mercy and show to compassion to whom I choose to show compassion.

24) The first commandment is: Thou shall love the Lord with all your heart, mind, soul and strength, and love thy neighbor as thyself. If you do indeed share in this commandment, then the other commandments would hopefully not flow out of you either because as a child of the Father, you wouldn't want to lie, cheat, steal, commit adultery, murder, covet or curse anyone. You would and should love them.

25) In today's world we should treat everyone as brothers or sisters, because we just don't know who is or isn't a part of the Family of Faith. Until we find out otherwise, even then, we shouldn't be unkind to them or treat them as any less than us, but rather see them as someone who may one day give up their wicked ways and come home to the Father, and join the rest of us in being part of this great, awesome and loving Family that our loving Holy Father has created, so that His Glory may shine on us.

26) If God is the Father, and Jesus is the Son, and we are in the son then the Father calls us children and the Son calls us brothers and sisters. If that is true then if the Father is in the Son and the Son is in the Father; and if the Son is in us, and we are in the Son that means that we are in the Father, and the Father in us. God the Father, God the Son, and God the Spirit all three live inside us and that means we belong to something that the world cannot comprehend. Satan has blinded the eyes of the world so that the world cannot see or share in the Father's love.

27) We've all seen people with riches and power, especially when we think of royalty. Royalty represents money and power. The world knows and understands money and power (this way of thinking comes from the evil one). The world is greedy and wants to have it all, from the rich to the poor. Even an ungodly poor man will try to have power over those around him.

28) As children of the Faith, we are called to be better than that. Love is the currency of God and Grace is the Power. Christ showed His power by serving and showing Grace. He used His love to pay the ultimate price. By allowing Himself to be nearly beaten to death and then nailed to a cross and left to die. In Heaven, there is no currency. All of God's kingdom thrives in love. All His Kingdom supports one another. So too we must learn to do so here on Earth, as it is mentioned in the Lord's prayer "Let your will be done on Earth as it is in Heaven". Don't dream for riches or royalty but strive for Holiness because you now belong to a Holy Family, which is far better than any royal family.

29) Royalty is finite, while Holiness is infinite, without end. Royalty wants to rule over Holiness. It wants to set claims over it, but it cannot. Royalty is created by man, by evil works for evil works, to keep its riches and to rule over others and to make from them. Holiness is created by the Father, for the Father, and for His children. Anyone and everyone is invited to be a part of this Holy Family that is eternal.

30) Proverbs 22:27 speaks of how a man shouldn't lose his bed because he has no money to pay, and to give to those who ask of you. When your enemy is hungry, give him food to eat. All of this is scripture. When the Lord taught us the Lord's Prayer, he said: "Let your will be done on Earth as it is in heaven". This is very important, and unfortunately, I truly believe, most Christians don't get this.

31) All throughout the Bible, there is a common theme that we should all live by, a code of conduct, if you will. In Heaven there is no money, no rich and no poor. All are equal. All are children of God, and no one is in need of anything. All look out for and support one another. One huge, Holy Family, with billions of souls who are members of the Family. You are a member of the Family and so are many, many others in this world. You have Family all around you, and if they aren't Family, they are potential Family. Yes, even that person you may not

like so much. Scripture teaches us to love, bless, and pray for those who persecute you. You are not to return evil for evil, but to return evil with good works. Do not curse others with the same mouth you use to praise and honor God, your Father.

32) I am perfectly aware that Earth is not Heaven, but we can live in that Heavenly realm here on Earth as if we are in Heaven. That's how we are called to live, to be there for one another and to love one another. Our Lord and our Brother, Jesus, said: "They will know that you belong to me by How you love one another. And as I have loved you so too you must love one another". Our Lord also stated that we should not rule over one another like the Gentiles (lost) do.

33) In Acts 4:34 that there were no needy persons among them. Everyone in this community came together in such a way that His will was being done on Earth as it is in Heaven. If you should have a problem with this, maybe you should reevaluate your heart and the way you think about it. Prune your heart and compare your thoughts to the Father's will.

34) In the word community are two words comm and unity, come in unity, community. Are you following my thoughts here? Everyone in the community did a come-n-unity, they came together and agreed that not one person around them should be in need of anything.

35) I have seen and even experienced it myself a Christian property owner evicting a Christian renter because the renter is poor and thus is often late on rent. I've experienced Christians preferring the company of wealthy, non-believers over that of another believer, simply because the believer is poor. The poor are looked down upon. This is not good. Scripture is all about loving one another, helping one another, and showing mercy. Scripture speaks a lot about helping your poor brother. Our Lord Jesus said that He didn't come for the righteous, but for the sinners. He was often criticized for being a friend to sinners.

36) A man with much wealth came to Jesus and asked, "Lord what should I do to inherit eternal life?" Jesus replied, " Love the Lord thy God with all your heart, all your mind, all your strength. And love your neighbor as thyself". The man stated, "All these I have done, what do I still lack?" Here Jesus replied, "If you wish to be perfect, go and sell all your belongings then come and follow Me". The man went away sad because he had much. Jesus then said, "Because of this it is easier for a camel to go through the eye of a needle than for a rich man to enter the kingdom of Heaven." Notice how the man responded when Jesus said to love your neighbor as yourself: All this I have done. The man lied. He didn't love his neighbor as himself. Remember what scripture said, if a man says he loves God but does not love his brother is a liar. The rich man didn't love his poor brother enough to help him.

37) There was a rich man who filled his barn with much, then said to himself: I have much goods stored up for myself to last me a long time and cared less for those in need around the corner. Because of this, the man died that day. God's will be done on Earth as it is in heaven.

38) There is absolutely no reason why anyone should be in need of anything. What does everyone need on Earth? Food, a home, clothes on their back, transportation to get around? The world throws away enough food in one day to feed the entire planet for a week. There are enough homes to go around. Clothing and transportation are plentiful. There is no reason for anyone to be without. However, because of greed, we will fill our own barn and neglect our poor neighbor. If it is in your power to help someone who is struggling in any way, then it is your responsibility to help the person in need.

39) Paul wrote that if a man knowing what is good and yet does not do it, for him it is sin. Likewise, if you see someone who is in need, and know that you are able to help and yet you do not help the man, whatever his situation, for that is a sin for you. You have turned a blind eye to the one in need and refused to help. This is not loving your

neighbor as yourself. You have decided not to share the blessing given to you, so you can share with others but instead kept it for yourself, perhaps for use at a later time.

40) There is a wonderful joy and blessing that comes from expressing that kind of love. Let me ask you, if you had a bank account in Heaven and the only way you can make a deposit is by what you give away on Earth, what would you part with? How much would you give away? In a sense, you do have an account in Heaven. Scripture speaks a lot about rewards given to those who do good works. Ministering to others comes in many different ways, not only spiritual.

41) Keep in mind our Lord Jesus had another reason why he came. Jesus said, "I did not come to be served, but to serve." A king who serves the people? Wow! Has there ever been a worldly king who traded his riches for rags and to serve the needy? Only one, but He wasn't of the world, though He was born into the world. He was not of the world but indeed had overcome the world and focused on His Father's Kingdom trying to teach us how to do the same by following Him.

42) The Lord usually uses other people that He has blessed to bless you. He also wants to bless others through you. Imagine that you're sitting at the table with Jesus and others. He has one cup in His hands, filled with blessings. Then He says take a drink and pass it on. Would you be greedy and try to take a big drink or just a sip and pass it on?

43) We should show the love of the Father by sharing His love and blessings. Remember that everyone is a potential fellow brother or sister. I cannot say that enough and it's all through scripture, and especially through the New Testament. It's all about love. For as the Holy Father first loved us, so too we must love one another. The New Testament teaches us a lot. It shouldn't be difficult to understand. If you truly seek the Father, then He and He alone will reveal His

secrets. To seek Him, is a secret in itself. That's how you get to know the Father, by seeking Him.

44) Learn the Holy Bible, read the Holy scriptures and meditate on them day and night. Listen to Christian music, sing worship songs, and pray. Scripture says to pray daily, and to pray without ceasing. Scripture also says that our spirit will pray for us even when we don't know the words to say. Wow! Not only can God, our Father, hear our silent prayers but He even hears the prayers of our spirit that our own ears can't hear. The Father hears our prayers even when we don't know we are praying. Wow, wow, wow is all I can say.

45) Let me be the first to admit, I am not a big reader. Although you wouldn't think that by looking at my collection of books. My whole library is about scripture. I can say I have read all of some and some of all. But the first time I read the Bible, it took me three years, reading for hours, day in and day out. I wasn't reading for speed. I was reading for understanding, and I don't like to read. I bought so many books to help me on my journey. I have enough notes to write another book. I learned a lot those first few years and continue to learn. These last couple of years have been overwhelming with what our Father has shared with me.

46) One thing I know is true. None of us will ever stop growing spiritually. The Father will always have something new to show you that He's there. Seek Him. However, all that wisdom, knowledge, and understanding means nothing if I don't love and to live it and share it.

47) Our Father, our Holy Father, our Heavenly Father, our one and only Father, is like a Father who started up a Family business. His business is the business of saving souls. He wants to save souls because He loves them. He loves our souls. He created us; therefore, we are His creation, His children. So, we are in on the job training, out in the field and we learn as we go. Train and over time you will become filled with

experience. It will start to become natural, like second nature, to just be and do good.

48) So, to be in the Family, is to also work in the Family business, learn your calling and take your place. Your job is to love one another, to be there for one another, to care for one another, as scripture states. If one suffers, we all suffer. If one is lifted, we are all lifted.

49) We have a tendency to turn a blind eye when we see someone who is in need or struggling. This is not good; in fact, it is evil. Scripture states that if a man knows what is good and does not do it, for him it is sin. It says to help those who are in need because you may be the hand of God at that moment. You may be the blessing your Father is sending to bless another child, your brother or sister who is in need.

50) What does it mean when our Lord said He has overcome the world? Is He saying that we too must learn to overcome the world? I've heard people say, well God wants us to prosper. Although I do agree, I do not agree in a worldly sense but in a spiritual one. He wants us all to prosper in Him. I know Christians who take from the poor when they cannot pay. Christians who have other Christians arrested or evicted. When God asks you "why were you so harsh with your brother when he could not pay?" What are you going to say? Sorry God it was just business? Remember the separation of the goats and the lambs. Remember the Lord's prayer, "let thy will be done on Earth as it is in Heaven".

51) Do you want to see the world change? Then, start by being that change. Remember what our Lord told us, "that the world will know that you belong to Me by How you love one another". By How we love one another.... Don't just show the world you're a Christian by wearing a cross or going to church but by how you love others. Love your enemy. Love your neighbor as yourself. Your neighbor is anyone in need. Therefore, hate the evil, for in the end it will be destroyed. Love

those who don't know the Father. Showing the Father's love to those who don't know God can and will pull them to the Father.

52) In the book of Jonah, God called Jonah to go to that great city, Nineveh, to call out against it, for their sins had gone up before the Lord. Jonah resisted the Lord's call. Not because he didn't want them to die, but rather it seems to be the opposite. Jonah knew that the Lord was merciful and forgiving. He knew that if he did deliver the message of destruction to Nineveh and they were to repent from their wickedness, that God would relent of His destruction and save that nation. I'm not sure why, but this upset Jonah (from my personal understanding the Jewish people did not like to share God with outsiders). This made Jonah so angry, he wanted to die. At the end of the short book, Jonah was more concerned for the plant that God made to grow and die in one day, then concerns for the two hundred thousand souls, who, as God put it, didn't know their left from their right. Where was Jonah's love for the lost?

53) Most Jews or Israelites didn't care about all the souls outside of their own nation. As a matter of fact, they rejected them, even though throughout their own scriptures God speaks about how He goes throughout all the Earth, searching every heart and mind. Scripture also spoke about how God used many people who were not of Israel descent to do His will in Israel. Even Abraham was a pagan man and many other non-Israelites who played major roles in the birth of Jesus. Melchizedek, who was a priest of God in which Abraham had given a tenth of what he had to him. Rahab of Jericho, who gave birth to Boaz, who married Ruth in so making both women outsiders. This made their children Samaritans, which the Jewish and Israelite people would come to hate simply because they were mixed. In return, through them and the line of David comes Jesus.

54) Some of the prophets, as well, spoke of people outside of Israel that would have a chance to find God's love. Solomon also prayed to God

that if any man who is to set his eyes toward Israel, the Temple, and called out to God, that God would hear their prayers and save them. Yet most of Israel and the Jewish nation would turn a blind eye to the souls outside of their nation, of the world. God told Israel not to be like the world. Israel wants to be like the world and have God but not want the world to have God.

55) Israel was supposed to have been a light to the world. They did the exact opposite. However, God would still use their evil acts to shine His light on the world. God would take again, what man meant for evil God would use for His good. Through Israel, and a few Gentiles, would come Jesus and through Jesus comes God's light, love and grace to the world.

56) For those of us who accept Christ as our Lord, if we don't share that same grace and love for the lost then we are still of the world and not of Jesus. We still haven't laid down our own greedy desires and picked up our cross to follow Jesus. Follow Jesus and His example of sharing the Father's love.

57) What if salvation was only for the Jews? Some still believe that. Where would we be today? We would not be saved and have no hope! That's not a good feeling and unfortunately some people do have that feeling. Thanks to God, the Father, and His love through His Son, our Brother, Jesus our Lord and King: There is hope for an eternal salvation. There is a chance for every soul on Earth to be saved, a chance for the world to be saved.

58) In 1 John 4:20 it is written that if a man says he loves God but hates his brother, he is a liar. For if he loves not his brother of whom he can see, he cannot love God of whom he has not seen. This goes back to what we recently discussed about how important it is to love your neighbor, your brother as yourself. A love so great that it changes the whole world. John writes in his Gospel 13:31-38 that Jesus said: "A new commandment I give you that you love one another. By this all

people will know you are my disciples. If you have love for one another, remember all these loves. For love covers a multitude of sins."

Reading Scripture

I really cannot stress enough about the importance of reading and studying scripture, the Holy Bible. In one sense the words Holy Bible can be understood with   the

Holy

One

Leaves

You

Basic

Instructions

Before

Leaving

Earth

2) Like I mentioned before, I don't like to read. However, I do because I want to learn our Father's will. And I learn a lot by constantly studying scripture. I really love it when the Father teaches me a revelation while I am deeply pondering His word. Ever since I was young, I've felt the Father's calling on my life. However, like many others, I allowed the world to pull me in and pull me in it did. Many years later, our Father started to call on me to come back. Like so many others, I was like the prodigal son, who after partying his life away, started to remember my Father in Heaven, and started a long journey back to my Heavenly Father.

3) I found a church, by accident. I wasn't looking. However, I felt the Father pulling me back in. A few months later, I received two DUIs in less than a month and went to jail for a few months and then to rehab. I didn't like it. However, I knew I needed it. I knew I had a drinking problem. I realized shortly after that I needed that to happen. I believe that was the Father's way of saying to me, "Son, you have a problem and you can't do the work I have for you while you're living this way". I would like to say that it all stopped right then but it didn't. It did get better and that was a start. It was a long journey to recovery. I can say that today I am freed from that sickness.

4) One night I was at a bar and by this time I felt God's calling on my life. I had started reading the Bible. (God calls us all to ministry in some form or another. As the Father gives to us, so too we must give to those in need. Remember scripture, because you don't know if God is using you as His hand at work in the other person's life, perhaps this was one of those moments). Let's go back to the bar.... While I was there, I met a guy. I don't remember his name. I do remember he was up here from Texas on business. I've often wondered what would bring someone from Texas to my small town in Tennessee. We talked mostly about scripture and God. I had started my journey in scripture in Genesis and was in Numbers or Deuteronomy, don't remember which now. When we were leaving, the guy offered me a ride home. I accepted the ride, I was buzzing pretty good by this time. Once home, we talked a lot more about scripture. The guy asked me to stop reading where I was at in the Bible and go to the New Testament. He asked me to start in John, or at least Acts, then straight through to Revelation. Then he wanted me to go back to Matthew, Mark, and Luke. After all that, I should go back to Genesis and start the Old Testament. That would take me the next three years, hours every day, day in and day out, to get completely read through the Bible my first time reading it. I went back to school in a sense, but with God as my teacher.

5) Jesus said in Matthew 23:4-10, "Call no man on Earth Father. For you have but only one Father who is in Heaven. Neither be called teachers, for you only have one teacher, the Christ". I don't read because I enjoy it. I read to learn about God the Father, and His will, His true mercy, His true love. His love for us now and His will for us. I read to learn how to love Him and to love one another as Christ loved us. Because Christ loved us, we must love one another and love our neighbor as our self.

6) During this journey I would start reading and in about thirty minutes to an hour, my table would be full of other books to help me to better understand what I was reading. Now it is sixteen years later, I'm still studying, still reading, and still learning to continue to constantly ponder on God as the Father, as my Father, as our Father, and what He has to say in His word. I ponder on His will, His love for us and the love we should have for one another. To constantly grow in His love is to be constantly growing in love for my neighbor, my brother and sister, my friend and for my enemy. We are to pray constantly for this kind of love to be given to us. Jesus said not to just love those who love you, for even the gentiles do this but to have a greater love. Not only receive the love of the Father but to share the Father's love with the world.

7) If I've said it once, I'll say it a million times, never forget what our Lord said, "The world will know you belong to Me by How you love one another". So also, we should constantly pray for His wisdom, His knowledge, His understanding and that of scripture.

8) While I was writing this, I just heard on the radio, "If you are more fortunate than others, build a longer table not a taller fence". Wow, what truth.... Seek to be a tool in God's tool box. Never forget, you are a part of the family. You are a child of God. As a family member, we all are part of the Father's family business. With that we all have a job to do. Be a tool in the Father's hand and let Him be in control of you, His tool.

9) At times it takes more than one particular tool to get a job done. If the job is too big for one tool, then ask the Father for more tools, more brothers and sisters to help you with the mission, the job you're on. Let the Father put His hand on you and use you to do His will, to share His grace. Share His love to anyone who is willing to listen, hear and receive, even to those who don't know they need to listen, hear and receive, mainly the lost. We are to love them, the lost, with that kind of love. We are to love them in such a way as to want to share our blessings. It is the kind of love that is soul saving, the kind of love that wants to build the Family of God, the Holy Family of the Holy Father.

10) I have made it to a point in my life where God, and God's word and will, are constantly on my mind, day and night. At times, some things that shouldn't may pass through my mind. When that happens, I have to stop, remember I'm a child of the Holy Father, and those are not acceptable thoughts. They are not loving, kind, graceful, or merciful thoughts. I have to immediately cast it out and ask my Father for mercy because evil thoughts have crossed my mind. This is spiritual growth. James 1:15 speaks about sin in the mind. When sinful thoughts enter our mind, sin is conceived and when the thoughts are put into words or actions, you have just given birth to sin and sin will lead to death.

11) Our Father does not want His children to die in their sins but to live in His eternal grace. He wants to show us His love, to share His love with us. He loved us enough to send His beloved Son, to show us how we should love one another, so that we may not see death, but live. I try to spend as much time as I can either studying and pondering on the Father's word and will or singing worship and songs of praise to our Father and remembering to give thanks for everything.

12) In case you're wondering, I'm not a singer or performer of any kind. I did come from a "rocker" background but now it's Christian and Worship music all the way. I do prefer new contemporary worship. That's just my preference, not everyone's. Everyone who is a

child of God must remember the scripture says to give a sacrifice of praise. Using the fruit of the lips, our words to give praise to God in all things: with such sacrifice the Lord is well pleased. Sometimes when I'm in a quiet situation where it's just me and the Father, I'll do what some would call freelance music, put some words together from my own heart, mind and soul and sing praises.

13) In my line of work, I'm able to have listen to audio most of the time. With modern day technology and probably the best thing I love about my phone is the radio app and my Bible app. If I'm not listening to worship music, I'm listening to the Bible being read to me in which I can complete the whole Bible in just a couple of weeks. I do highly recommend the app BIBLE.IS. I use the standard English, dramatized version. It's really cool. With every character having their own voice, it is like having it presented in the form of a television program but without the visual. It really brings the story to life. The app is an amazing tool. If you're like me and don't like to read, or don't read fast, unlike my wife who could read the whole Bible in less than a week, (It takes me months to read it myself....Grrr...LOL), listening to the word and worship as I work is a great blessing.

14) It's important to know that the Father searches hearts and minds of all humans, so let us ponder on His love, His grace, His word and all things Godly. In a sense, this is one way to be in constant prayer. I strongly encourage learning the scriptures in any way you can. Remember to pray about it as well. Don't read for speed but for depth and understanding.

PRAYER

Prayer is everything, even with scripture. Ask your Father to reveal His mysteries to you. Jesus often went off to be alone to pray. Our Lord often prayed for blessings, He prayed for us and His disciples. He prayed over the food, to give thanks and for the Father's blessings of food and for those who ate of the food. He taught us to give thanks for all things. Jesus disciples even ask Him how they should pray. Our Lord Jesus, our Brother taught His disciples (His brothers and sisters, our brothers and sisters) to pray like this:

Our Father who is in Heaven,

Hallowed be your name.

Your Kingdom come, your will be done,

On earth as it is in Heaven.

Give us this day our daily bread.

Forgive us our trespasses, as we forgive those who trespass against us.

Lead us not into temptation, but deliverer us from evil.

For yours is the kingdom, and the power, and the glory, forever and ever.

AMEN.

2) I have learned to apply this in my own prayers every morning before I leave my house. I do this for a few reasons. As I do this it helps me to remember the Father's will for how we are to treat one another, as we go about our day.

3) I know there are a lot of books out there about the Lord's prayer. For me though, I use it like this: First one needs to know what HALLOWED means. it means to make Holy, let it be Holy, it is Holy or simply put, His Name is Holy forever and ever AMEN.

4) The next section talks about the Kingdom of God and His will being done on earth as it is in heaven. I pray this for all of us - His children. This is how we should all live, act, respond, help and love as if we are already in Heaven. In a sense we are, in a sense God's Kingdom is where He is and His kingdom is where His children are. Make it your job to start your day to live a Kingdom day. If you fall short, stop and pray. Then aim to do better. Recognize that each and every person you lay your eyes on is either a brother and sister or a potential brother and sister then treat them like that because they really are.

5) At the same time remember that most are far from the Lord. So treat everyone as if they are brothers and sisters even if you know they are not. Seek to know if they are not, so that you may find an opportunity to plant a seed and perhaps lead them to the Lord and save a lost soul. Deny no-one an opportunity to be saved. If they refuse to listen that's ok, just know that you've done your best to lead a lost soul to the Lord. At least you will have planted a seed in their hearts. The scripture tells us that one plants, another waters but the Lord gives it the growth. It also says: many are called but only a few will be chosen.

6) Our Father is so great and loving, that although all humans are sinful, and no one is without sin He must have seen some good in us to give us the possibility of hope. A love so great should not be treated lightly. We can get a sense of how great His love for us is when we read the scripture that God says: "I have no delight in the death of a wicked man but that the wicked man would turn from His wicked ways and do good. To come to me with his whole heart and I would heal him." No matter how bad a person is, there's hope. God desires that we love Him with

all of our heart, mind, soul and strength and to love all with all that we have.

7) Many years I've spent training myself in changing the way I think, speak and live. I've learned to see people with a different set of eyes: As brothers and sisters or potential brothers and sisters yet understanding that most are not. At one time I use to look at women as a sex objects, I would check them out as they would walk by me. Now I can honestly say I'm freed from that evil as well. I know people, even Christians, who would say things like "its ok to look as long as you don't touch" for me that is a lie as well. Jesus said in Matthew 5: 28 that whoever looks at a woman with lustful intent has committed adultery with her in his heart. Now I see them as a sister even if they're not. We can't tell who is or isn't a part of the Family just by looking. By the way, would you look with lust at your earthly brother or sister? Of course not. It should be the same with your spiritual brothers and sisters, your eternal brothers and sisters. Keep your thoughts in check. Keep your eyes from getting set on things that would cause you to have sinful thoughts or say something sinful.

8) When the Lord's prayer comes to the part about give us this day our daily bread, I like to split it up into two different parts. I leave the first part is as it sounds. I ask the Father to give us all our daily bread, (bread for the body) today. I also ask our Father to remember the poor and the homeless; for all those who don't know where their next meal is going to come from. It is possible that it might be me that our Father wants to use me or us to provide food for another. Because the Father has used others to bless me and provide for me, I need to learn to let the Father use me to bless others and provide for others.

9) Second, I ask and pray that our Father would also provide us our daily bread for our soul. His bread of life and His living water. In John 6: 35 Jesus tells us, "I Am the Bread of Life. He that comes to Me shall never hunger and he that believes in Me shall never thirst." This is His

vary word and will. I pray this so that He will help us to do His will by doing good, by seizing every opportunity to serve Him as we serve others.

10) We are to love Him by serving others and we serve others because we love Him and are called to love the ones we serve. Like our Lord said: I did not come to be served but to serve. Jesus came to lead by example. Follow in His footsteps and seek to serve others in any way you are able. Serve spiritual food, which is your compassion, your love, mercy, time, money, energy, ear, words, and comfort. Whatever the form of feeding, feed the sheep. The only thing stopping you is you. Don't think about it, just do it.

11) Share your blessing with one who is in need of a blessing. Be that blessing that people need and you will be even more blessed. Be the blessing, it's your job. Scripture states that if you see a person in need and say: "be filled and blessed" and you do not give the man what is needed though you are able, then for that man it is sin. It's true, you have not done what was good and have sinned against your Father and your brother by rejecting him in his time of need, though you were able. Remember the separation of the goats and the lambs. When the Lord says to the Lambs, come enter the Father's Glory, for whatever you done for the least of these My Brothers you also did for Me. Then to the goats, depart from Me you who are wicked, for whatever you didn't do for the least of these My Brothers, you also didn't do for Me.

12) In the next section of the prayer different gospel writers use different words. Matthew says forgive us our debts and Luke says forgive us our trespasses. I like to use both because we need God to forgive us both of our sins and our debts. At the same time, we need to learn to forgive those who have sinned against us and also those who are in debt to us.

13) Because we are children of the Living Father, we must also apply this to our work, which for me means my business. All my clients owe

me for the work that I have done for them. The way I've worked it out is if someone doesn't want to pay me for the service I've provided, for any reason, I simply stop providing my service to them. I don't get mad, nor do I seek to get paid. Neither would I dare to try to take anything of theirs for payment. I will still love them and do whatever I can for them, I just won't do business with them any longer.

14) I also make it known to all my clients that I am a Christian. Like I said earlier, you never know who is or isn't a Christian. I've had the opportunity to share God's word and be a witness to someone who isn't a believer. I have also ministered and prayed with many who were. The best and most rewarding payoff is the feeling I get after ministering to someone when I'm out in the field doing my normal work. If I'm on the clock working and then I start to minister to someone all work comes to a stop. It's now time to minister to a brother or sister. In that moment my business clocks out and my Father's family business clocks in. Its soul saving and sheep feeding time. When that work is done, which I do not rush, it's time to get back to my normal job.

15) Scripture says we must not profit from our brothers and sisters. I labor with my hands and earn a living. I can earn a living without making a profit. Bills get paid and food is put on the table. However, it seems that as soon as I get a little money saved up, I either have to spend it on repairs or buy equipment. I put my full trust in our Father to provide for my household.

16) We must also learn to not curse people with the same lips we use to give thanks, honor and praise to our Heavenly Father. In James 3:9-10, it talks about how with our mouth we give praise to our Lord and Father but with the very same lips we curse others. We've all heard the expression; "do you kiss your mother with those lips?" when someone speaks in a foul manner. Likewise, I believe it should be said when one speaks evil against another, do you praise God with those lips?

17) Let me repeat verse 10 of James 3: From the same mouth comes both blessings and cursing. My brothers these things should not be done. In Psalms 62:4 we read: They praise me with their lips but curse me in their heart. Keep guard over your heart. Be careful not to curse others no matter what they may say or do. Jesus, never spoke evil against those who did Him harm. He wants us to follow His example. We also need to remember what our Father told Cain in Genesis: If you do good will you not be accepted? Sin is crouching at the door, waiting to devour you. You must overcome it!!! Likewise, in Luke 7:47 our Lord said, "Therefore I tell you, her sins, which are many, are forgiven, for this she loves much. But the one who is forgiven little, loves little".

18) We are called to walk in His ways and do good. We should desire that His will be done not ours if we are seeking to walk in the ways of the world. We need to learn to open our ears to hear the Spirit when He is speaking to your heart. If it's good, it's from the Spirit and the Spirit is a gift from the Father. As scripture puts it, anything that you receive that is good is a gift from the Father. At the same time the good gift that you give is a gift from the Father to the receiver.

19) Don't ignore the gifts given you by the Father but receive those gifts whether material or spiritual and use your blessings to bless others. If your cup is overflowing, then find someone with an empty cup and pour what's in your cup and into their cup, so that our Father can pour more into your cup. A cup can never be full as long as it is pouring out.

20) Another thing I like to add to my morning prayer is that our Father would cloth us with spiritual armor. In scripture that is called the Armor of God. The following are the various parts of armor that scripture talks about:

The belt of truth,
The breast plate of righteousness,
Sandals to deliver the gospel of peace,
The shield of faith,

The helmet of salvation.
And the sword of the Spirit

21) In Romans 13:14 Paul tells us "To put on the Lord Jesus Christ". What he means is that Jesus is our armor. We need to imitate Him so that we can be like the Father's beloved Son, our Brother. We need to learn to love as He has loved us, to walk as He walked, to talk as He talked. What that means is that we should strive to keep the first two commandments: love the Lord your God with ALL you heart, mind, soul and strength. And love your neighbor as yourself. Unlike other commandments that tell us not to do things. These are commands to do. When we don't love God and our neighbor we are in sin.

22) We've all been told that if we lie, cheat, steal, commit adultery, covet, or dishonor our mother and father we're in sin. But you rarely hear that NOT loving your neighbor as yourself is a sin. Or that NOT loving God with all your heart, mind, soul and strength is a sin. Love your neighbor as you love yourself in the same way the Father, Jesus and the Spirt, love as they love themselves. Love the Father with all your heart, mind, soul and strength as Jesus loves the Father with all His heart, mind, soul and strength. We must follow our Lord and Brother to the Father, for He is the only way to the Father. Follow no other man but the one and only true Son of the Father to the Father. As Paul himself wrote telling us not to follow him for he was just a messenger. Rather we should all follow the Lord, Jesus Christ and in following our Lord, we should strive to be like our Father and walk in all His ways. We should also all be messengers and deliver the Gospel of peace as our Lord commanded him and us.

23) We are also to cloth ourselves with our Father's invisible armor. In other words, we are to be covered with Jesus our Lord and Brother, the Christ. In doing this we will be strengthened in the spirit by the power and might of our Lord. It's like this: The Father is in the Son and the Son is in the Father. Therefore, if you are in the Son then the Son is in

you then you are also in the father and the father is in you. This is how you can be able to stand against the evil one.

24) Practicing your faith is like someone that buys a piano but doesn't know how to play it. They need to go out and find a teacher to show them how to play and then they have to actually sit down and try to do what they've been taught on their new piano. In time they will get better and better, until eventually they learn to play the piano. At the same time knowing there will always be something new to learn, something new to play. It's the same way with your faith. The more you practice it, the stronger it gets, the more you learn the more powerful you will become. We all have the power and strength of Christ; we just need to set our heart and mind on the Lord. As the Lord said: According to your faith so shall it be. In all of this we must set our hearts and minds fully on the Father and His Son. Let God be your only Father and His Son your Teacher through the power of the Holy Spirit. Continue to practice your faith and works with love and watch what the Father will do with your faith.

25) On top of praying to be clothed with God's spiritual armor, I also pray that our Father will surround us with His hedge of protection as it says in Job 1:10, "Have you not put a hedge of protection around him and his family?" And also, in Psalm 91which is a prayer of protection. I ask in prayer for our Father to protect us every day.

26) Remember to always give the Father all the thanks, honor and glory, to Him who loved us and provides for us in ways we cannot even begin to understand. Keep in mind also how He uses others to serve you. At the same time be aware that God wants you to serve others, becoming more like our Lord Jesus in the way that He didn't come to be served but rather came to serve others. For instance, at the last supper He served His disciples and as He was serving them He said: "The Son of man did not come to be served but to serve...Let those who are to be great among you also be a servant." Our call is to be like our

Lord, be a servant and serve. Be like the greatest King who has ever lived and walked on this earth. One who was born of God and man. Be like the one and only true King and follow Him. He calls us to do that very thing: "Come and follow me". Unlike other worldly kings who wanted to be served by others, our King served others and still does. As He serves us His brothers and sisters we should also serve.

27) I have chosen a place outside of my home where I meet with the Father every morning before I leave for work. I decided to do this years ago since at the time I did not have a closet in my home big enough to use. Last year while reading another book by Jonathan Cahn, called The Book of Mysteries, there was a place in it where the student asked the teacher if the Holy of Holies still existed? The teacher said yes, it's that place where you meet God every day. So, in a since, this place is my Holy of Holies. As Jesus told us we need to go into the inner room of our house and pray in secret. This special place where you meet with your heavenly Father, the place where it's just you and Him – that is your Holy of Holies. You can pray at any time at any place. But that one place is your Holy place.

28) You can pray anywhere at any time and for any reason. You can pray while you're driving, working, playing or doing anything. If the Lord puts someone or something on your mind, then pray about it. Talk with your Father as if He is standing right next to you or right in front of you. Several times in scripture it speaks about how some, like Moses, talked with God as one person speaks to another. We must follow by example. Speak to your Father as if He is right there, because He truly is.

29) Pray, pray, pray, then pray some more. Although it is good to speak with your Father with your voice, keep in mind that He also hears the prayers in your mind, in your heart and He also hears the prayers of your very soul. Remember, the spirit will pray even when we don't know what to say. Be in constant prayer, pray without ceasing.

Continually build your relationship with your Father. Like in everyday relationships if there is no communication there is no relationship. The more you communicate with those around you, the stronger the relationship, the greater the bond you will have with them, the more your love for them will grow. It's the same with your Heavenly Father. At the same time help build your Father's house by building relationships with all of those God puts in your daily path.

30) In our everyday life we've all experienced what it is like to love our parents when we were children and even as adults. And most of us have experienced what it is like to have the love of being a parent to our children. Those types of love are drops in the bucket compared to how much God loves us. God the creator of love loved us first.

31) Let me be clear you don't have to pray like I pray. I'm just letting you know that you should pray. Scripture says to pray in all circumstances for all peoples and to give thanks for all things. Jesus also gave us an example to follow. Don't follow me; follow Jesus and His example. Follow all His ways. Follow Him and Him only. We can help lead the lost to Christ and feed His sheep, but He gives the growth. We should not expect them to keep following us but once to Christ we let go and let Christ grab them and pull them to Him.

32) Pray, speak to the Father about anything and everything, anyone and everyone. Ephesians 6:18 tells us to pray in the spirit on all occasions with all kinds of prayers and request. I recently heard a singer talk about something his pastor had said. He asked, if God answered the prayers you've been praying, would it change anyone's life other than your own? Wow, what a question.

33) Matthew 6:8 tells us that, our Father knows what we need before we ask Him. Again, in James 4:3 we read: you have not because you ask not. You ask and do not receive because you ask wrongly. To spend it on your own passions. The next verse says: "You adulterous people! Do you not know that friendship with the world is enmity with God?"

I believe this is something to remember while praying. I believe that when we speak to the Father on behalf of another person with love, our Father puts His ear a little closer simply because you have expressed concern and love for your brother or sister and even for the one who doesn't yet know the Lord. He delights in you seeking to save their soul because of your love, mercy and compassion for them. Just as you also were a sinner, a sojourner and as the Father has shown you love, mercy and compassion, we too must follow our Lord and do the same.

34) Scripture speaks a lot about unity. There is power in unity. Jesus said, "Where two or three are gathered in My name in one accord then I AM there in the mist of them." Jesus is the Holy Son of the Holy Father. We are His children and He calls on us to be holy and righteous. In fact, He commanded us to be holy and righteous just like He is. Jesus also says, "you shall be perfect as the Father is perfect." Learn to live a perfect life so you can learn to live righteously. Learn to live a righteous life so you can learn to live a Holy life. Learn to live with one another as true brothers and sisters because that's what we are: children of God the Father and brothers and sisters to our Lord and Brother Christ Jesus. Learn to live with one another here on earth as if you are already in heaven. God's kingdom is where is children are. In doing this you can and will learn how to truly live.

35) Remember that the disciples continued to grow while walking with our Lord. However, Thomas, one of the twelve, didn't fully believe till after His resurrection. After the Lord ascended to the Father, He sent His helper the Holy Spirit to them filling them with power so that they able to continue the work the Lord had called on them to do in His name: Teaching, healing, preaching, evangelizing and ministering to others. We are called to do likewise. Jesus often asked, "do you believe I can do this?" and often the reply was "Yes Lord I believe". Then the Lord would say, "According to your faith, so shall it be done for you." This is how it should be for us too.

36) I have personally experienced God saying yes to my requests, but I've also heard no. I've received a yes to prayer in ways that only God's mighty power could have done. I have also received many no's. Some of the those that I have received were probably because it would affect me or someone else in a negative way and might cause someone to fall astray. Perhaps the Lord was trying to save us from something, because He knows if we are weak and not strong enough to handle the load in a righteous way. Certainly, we may think we are strong enough to handle the situation, but God knows us better than we know ourselves. He knows our weaknesses and He knows our strength's.

- 37) For instance, what about some of those aches and pains in my body? I know and believe in His healing power; I know it's real. With my own eyes I've seen it happen. So why doesn't He heal me? At least that's the way I thought about it. Then I remembered Paul. He struggled with a suffering that he described as a thorn in his side put there by satan to torment him. Little did satan know that God allowed this for building Paul up, to make a weak man strong in the Lord. Paul didn't realize it at the time because he said: "I spoke with the Lord a few times concerning this matter and the Lord said to me, My Grace is sufficient for you". It's the same way for us healing or not his grace is sufficient for us.

38) We should also keep in mind that there can be a blessing in suffering. A good example of this is Job. The scripture tells us that Job was a righteous man before the Lord. Satan incited God against Job saying, let me inflict him and bring harm to him and he will curse you to your face. But Job remained strong and faithful to the Lord and did not curse the Lord. Even Job's own wife said to him, "After all this do you still hold fast your integrity? Curse God and die". Job had suffered a lot. He had in one day lost all his herds and flocks, he lost all of his sons and daughters. As if this wasn't enough, he received sores and boils all over his body.

39) In the midst of these troubles his best friends (not to mention his wife) were no encouragement at all. Through all this hardship and suffering Job remained faithful to God. In the end God blessed Job with a double portion of what he had. We should follow the examples of Job and the Disciples and remain faithful all the way to the end, no matter how good or bad it gets, no matter your situation good or bad, hold on to Jesus for dear life.

40) The scriptures say: I will be to him a Father and he will be to me a Son. If he sins, I will punish him, as a father punishes his children because he loves them, to correct their ways. It's the same in our lives, the Father sometimes has to correct us and bring us back in line with His ways. I don't know about you, but I'd rather have His punishments here on earth then to lose my faith and suffer His everlasting punishments in the eternal lake of fire from which there is no rescue. That notion fills me with fear.

41) From my understanding of scripture, it is the fear of the Lord, which is the beginning of Wisdom. As Isaiah put it in chapter 11 of his book referring to Jesus: "His delight shall be in the fear of the Lord." In another place we are told that the one in whom the Lord delights, He will discipline in love that we may be strengthened to be like His Son and become one with Him. In being one with the Son we also become one with the Father as our Lord prayed for us to be. Through my afflictions I pray that I will come closer to the Father.

42) If you look at the world around us you can see that it is usually the children who never received punishments from their parents that lack respect for their parents, for themselves and for others. However, more often than not the child who received punishments out of love from the parent grows up to respect their parents. This is a commandment with a promise. Children honor your mother and father that it may go well with you. Unlike the child most of the time the parent knows what is best for the child. Knowing and understanding this helps me in my

growth and relationship with our Father. It also teaches me to stay strong and to put all my trust in our Holy Father. Talk to your heavenly Father as you would your earthly father and even more so, for, He is your True Father. Keeping in mind that your Father knows what is best for you. Maybe what you're asking for isn't what's best for you. It could cause more problems for you and perhaps for those around you. If God does say yes, then consider those He may use to get to you.

43) It is written: The God's thoughts are not humanity's thoughts, and humanity's thoughts are not God's thoughts. His understanding is not anything like the understanding of humanity. My pastor always says, "Righteous thinking produces righteous living". If that is true, we should meditate on righteousness day and night. That is a form of loving God with all our mind. In giving God all your mind, you will know how to think and live righteously. Do this and watch the growth the Father has in store for you. As it is written: One plants, another waters but God gives it the growth.

44) As a child continues to be under the care of their parents, they should be growing, learning and building a trust relationship with them. Building relationships with all those in the household should be a given. Loving one another and building solid relationships with all those in the household is essential. Loving one another, being there for one another, even for the one who seems to stir up trouble. Yet we should still show love for the whole family. We may hate their words or actions, yet we still love them.

45) Talk with your Heavenly Father, with a pure heart and build on your relationship with your Father. Live as if your house is your Father's house, cause after all, it is all His. Live in your Father's house and kingdom as if you were already there, because in a since you are. As its written, "Let your will be done on earth as it is in heaven. We should therefore, live on earth as if we were already in heaven. As our

Lord said: "The kingdom of God is in you and near you." The Kingdom of God is where His children are and in those who do His will.

46) As you pray for the world to change; the change starts in you. Be the change. Show the world you belong to Jesus, the Family of God and the Father by demonstrating your love to one another. Show the world how to love in Christ. Love others as Christ loves you. Demonstrate your love to Jesus by the way you show love and mercy to others, to the least of these, as He taught us. If Christ is indeed in you and you are indeed in Him, then live as if Christ is in you and you are in Him: Embrace it, receive it, live it and share it. You never know when your Father is testing you, to see what you will do, to see where your heart truly is as He uses you as a tool in His hand in order to bring good works in someone else's life as an answer to their prayers. God continually tests us to see if we will help others with what He has given us to use. He wants to test your heart and see if your giving because you need to or is it because you want to. Are you doing because you have to or does it come from your heart? We need to make sure that we are tool that is fit to do the work and not one that is broken.

47) Keep in mind that when you pray, the Father sends to you who and what you need. When someone else prays, God might send you or me or someone else to go help the one in need that is praying. We must remember the Lord's words "Whatever you did for the least of these my brothers, you also done unto me." Be a true brother or sister to all. Then watch your Father work His wonders and witness His mighty hand at work. You will witness prayers answered, both yours and theirs.

If you are one who wonders if your prayers are being heard. Look at what the Angel, our brother Gabrel told his brother and our brother Daniel. He said to him, "Don't worry Daniel, ever since you set your heart to know the Lord, your prayers have been heard. I hope this encourages your faith as it has mine.

MARRIAGE

In this chapter I'll speak of my own experiences in accordance with scripture. Scripture speaks a lot on the topic of marriage. Like David I have made my fair share of mistakes in this area. Even worse I did these things after I became a Christian and I knew better than to do it. I knew better, but I still chose to walk a wicked path and listen as satan whispered in my ear: "come over here, the grass is greener" It was a lie. I pray you learn from me and don't fall into that same trap. It certainly caused a world of sin. It will lead you into a world of trouble and destruction.

2) My wife and I have been through a lot. I cheated on her and she cheated on me. I left her for another woman and she left me for another man. We have children that she calls: his, mine and ours. We've been through the party stages. We've split up and gotten back together many times over. We have been married over 12 years and together over 22 years. From the last break up, we've been back together for over 4 years. But this time, I'm all in. I have to be. I need to be.

3) After much soul searching, the Father has opened my eyes to reality. I have learned what damage breaking the marriage vow can and will cause. I have made a commitment to both my wife and my heavenly Father, with regard to this sin, by His grace I will never commit this sin again. Not only will I by the grace of God never act upon this sin again, I will by that same grace keep it from my heart and thoughts. When it does try to cross my mind or heart, I will immediately cast it out and pray to the Father for His mercy. It takes time and trust. If you have true love, the kind of love that comes from the Father, you can work through anything. That's what we did.

4) For several years it was back and forth. I was still blinded. I reached a point where I realized that as long as I was living the way I was, my

heavenly Father was no longer with me. That my brothers, was a very painful reality. It hurt me to my very core. It felt as if God had left me and that whole in my soul that only He can fill seemed empty once again. I was alone, dying in my own sinful desires. I was at the end of my rope. I had to choose to let go and fall completely into my sin or turn from my wicked ways back to the goodness of God. I would have to look to Christ and ask for help. I needed to ask Him to please save me from my sinful path.

5) After much prayer begging for His mercy, He opened my eyes and I just broke down. Not just once or twice but several times. I needed something else more than brokenness. Like a vase being hit by a hammer and broken into pieces, I needed more, I needed the pieces to be broken into pieces. Even then that was not enough. I really needed all these to be smashed to smithereens. When God completely dealt with my sin, I could be put back together.

6) It was kind of like I was a cheap mass-produced vase that was deliberately broken and then reformed with pure gold. The old is destroyed so that the new is a one of a kind masterpiece a million times more valuable than the original was. This is what my Father had to do to me. And not just to me, but to my marriage. It had to be broken so that it could be restored and be more cherished than ever.

7) What I meant for evil God used for good. What I tried to destroy, our loving Father saved. Not only saved but rebuilt so as to make it stronger. I had to truly learn what it meant to put God first in my life. Constantly pondering on His ways, His love, and how He wants us to love each other. He began to show me the kind of love we all need in our marriages: Love, mercy, peace, grace.

8) Before my wife and I got back together this last time, I thought long and hard about it. I prayed about my marriage. I also prayed for the Father to change me. I needed a new heart, a new mind, a renewed spirit. If there was to be a change, the change would have to start with

me. I would have to be the change for my marriage to change. The biggest and most important change would be to put my Father first in my marriage, in my life and in all that I do.

9) A few pieces of key scripture kept crossing my mind. Matthew 18: 21-22, How many times should we forgive our brother, seven times? The Lord said, Not just seven times but seventy times seven, even all in the same day. If the one who sinned against you repents, you must forgive him every time. That goes for your spouse who sins against you as well. Men your wife is also your sister in the Lord and women your husband is your brother in the Lord. In the Father's Kingdom there is no one given in marriage (as in Mathew 22:30) but we will be like the angels. All are brothers and sisters in His kingdom, with Christ as our oldest Brother, God as our only Father. To truly love them is to also truly forgive them. Do we not sin against God daily? Scripture teaches us that we do on some level. Either by action, words, thoughts or even by our very heart. Yet do you still not ask for the Father's mercy and forgiveness? Yes, we all do and He gives it willingly. Therefore, then we must do to others.

> In 1 Corinthians 7 Paul writes: [10] Now to the married I command, *yet* not I but the Lord: A wife is not to depart from *her* husband. [11] But even if she does depart, let her remain unmarried or be reconciled to *her* husband. And a husband is not to divorce *his* wife... [16] For how do you know, O wife, whether you will save *your* husband? Or how do you know, O husband, whether you will save *your* wife?

10) Then, there is the love chapter in chapter 13 in 1 Corinthians. The whole chapter is important, but I apply verses 4-8 directly towards my marriage:

> [4] Love is patient and kind; love does not envy or boast; it is not arrogant[5] or rude. It does not insist on its own way; it is not irritable or resentful; [6] it does not rejoice at wrongdoing but rejoices with the truth. [7] Love bears all things, believes all

things, hopes all things, endures all things. [8] Love never ends...

11) There were several more verses that pushed me to repentance as well. Matthew 19:8, our Lord said, "Because of the hardness of your heart, Moses gave you the right to divorce your wives, but only on the grounds of adultery but in the beginning, it wasn't so." This hit me very close to home. For me to divorce my wife means I have no mercy, no forgiveness, no true love for my wife, my sister. If the Lord is to show me mercy, forgiveness and love, then I too must do the same for my wife. I must show her love, mercy and forgiveness.

12) Remember God's love, not man's love. God's understanding, not man's understanding, I had to let God back in my heart and give Him full control. I have to trust fully in His ways and to know that they are good and righteous. Man's ways are not good but evil. We must learn to understand His true love and apply it to our lives and to our marriages.

13) I have seen Christian families split up because of money. This is not good. I've seen a spouse leave and take the kids, because the other spouse lost their job and could no longer provide the type of lifestyle, they previously were able to live. At the same time, I've seen couples and families in true financial difficulties, flat broke and homeless, hold themselves together. The wife and kids still standing next to their husband and father in support. For better or for worse they stay together, wow. That is truly awesome. More often than not one spouse will leave another because of their short comings, whatever they may be.

14) We must remember our vows, for better or for worse, for richer or poorer, till death do us part. Remember the love you pronounced to one another. Do you truly love your spouse? If you were to lose everything tomorrow, would you still remain with your spouse? I enjoy meeting couples who have been together many years and struggled through

many hardships yet still have the same great love for one another as they did at first and maybe even more.

15) We sometimes have a hard time forgiving our spouse for their wicked acts or words (truly forgiving). Yet we all sin against God every day. No one is without sin. As scripture says, "God will not forgive you if you do not forgive others from your heart". God has clearly said that He desires mercy. God is our Father; we are His children. You, your spouse, your children and all that you have is His. Your spouse and your children are your brothers and sisters, because all of you are indeed His children.

16) As Christ is in the Father, and the Father is in Him, and as we are in Christ and Christ is in us, then in fact this means that your, your kids, your spouse and any other believer that you connect with in any way are joined with Christ and with the Father. Again, I repeat, as our Lord said, "Whatever you do to the least of these my brothers you also do unto me." It is also said that "Whatever you didn't do for the least of these my brothers you also didn't do for me".

17) When I look at my children, I don't just see them as my children but rather more like my younger brothers and sisters. I am to raise them for the Father. I am to teach them and guide them in the ways of the Father. As a good shepherd leaves the ninety-nine to go search for the one that is lost as to not give up on us when we wondered astray, so we must do as well. If your spouse has a problem, such as drugs, drinking, etc... You don't give up on the problem and leave. Just as you wouldn't want the Father to give up on you while you're in your sin. Have mercy for them and pray in the same way you would like for the Father to be patient with you. Again, I repeat scripture, how do you know wife if you will save your husband, or how do you know husband if you will save your wife?

18) A married couple are supposed to be a team supporting one another. The goal is to build the team, not to destroy it. To raise your children as

a team, as a family, as a family of God. For such you are. In scripture we read, "Men love your wives, wives respect your husbands." Why is this? Is it not because men show more respect than love and is it not because women show more love then respect? Let's be honest with ourselves! I don't think this would had been written if it weren't true. Again, we read, we should only let words of grace flow from our lips.

19) We should not curse others with the same heart, thoughts, or lips that we use to give our Father praise and thanksgiving. This is displeasing to our Father. Our Lord also taught us that if you have nothing nice to say then say nothing at all, not even in secret. For whatever you even say in secret will be brought to light. He even went so far to say watch your very thoughts. Think heavenly thoughts. It's bad enough to let evil in your thoughts but no matter what, do not let it leave your lips, the same lips you use to praise your Father. Pray for those who do evil. Show mercy so the Father will show you mercy. Jesus never returned evil with evil. And not once did He curse anyone who persecuted Him. Do not fall for the lies of the world that says, it's ok to divorce for any reason. This is a lie and leads to a world of sinful thoughts and actions, by both parties and from the other people involved.

20) Even while our Brother was hanging on the cross left to die (though He still lives) He prayed for those who put Him there. He prayed for His enemies who put Him on the cross, wow, that's love. If we are to follow His example and show this kind of love to our enemy, then how much more are we to love our spouses, our brothers and sisters, one another? Do we not constantly ask Him for His love, mercy and forgiveness? Then should we not show the same love, mercy and forgiveness to our spouse as we ask from our Father? Yes, we should.

21) Man, judges according to the sin. One sin seems worse than another to us. But in the eyes of the Father, a sin is a sin. No matter the sin, liars, thieves, murderers, adulterers, idolaters, all of them will end up in

the same place with the same punishment. However, there is hope for the sinful, hope for the lost. As the Father forgives your sins and leaves them in the past and remembers them no more, so to we must forgive our spouse (70 x7) daily, leave those sins where they lay, in the past remembering them no more. That also means, we shouldn't keep bringing old sins back up to be remembered.

22) In scripture Jesus calls satan "the father of lies." He is a master of leading people astray away from the Father and off the true path. Our call is to rebuke the enemy and cast him away in the power and authority of Jesus Christ through the power of the Holy Spirit.

23) Stay far away from adultery, don't even think about it. The grass may look greener on the other side, but it's a lie. If you stumble in this way there will be a lot of pain. Such sin causes a world of hurt. And this hurt is not just limited to you and your spouse but others around you. Some may be so hurt and angry that they call out to God to fight against you and curse your name.

24) Scripture says that if one divorces their spouse and remarry, that they are in sin. In fact, even the look of lust toward another is an act of adultery in your heart. My point in saying all of this is to try and keep you from disaster. Please don't let the world fool you into saying that there is nothing a wrong with looking, because that's how it all starts. Keep control of yourself, your heart, your mind and yes even your eyes.

25) Imagine for a second that you know that your relationship with your Heavenly Father is over. What if the Lord told you that He has had enough of your evil ways? And although you beg and plead for His mercy, He still says no! That is exactly what we do when we turn our backs to our spouse. Whether we leave them for someone else or we've just had enough of whatever their issues. It would be the end of love and mercy.

26) Remember there is a blessing that comes with suffering as 1 Peter 4:12-19 tells us:

> [12] Beloved, do not be surprised at the fiery ordeal among you, which comes upon you for your testing, as though some strange thing were happening to you; [13] but to the degree that you share the sufferings of Christ, keep on rejoicing, so that also at the revelation of His glory you may rejoice with exultation. [14] If you are reviled for the name of Christ, you are blessed, because the Spirit of glory and of God rests on you. [15] Make sure that none of you suffers as a murderer, or thief, or evildoer, or a troublesome meddler; [16] but if *anyone suffers* as a Christian, he is not to be ashamed, but is to glorify God in this name. [17] For *it is* time for judgment to begin with the household of God; and if *it begins* with us first, what *will be* the outcome for those who do not obey the gospel of God? [18] And if it is with difficulty that the righteous is saved, what will become of the godless man and the sinner? [19] Therefore, those also who suffer according to the will of God shall entrust their souls to a faithful Creator in doing what is right.

27) Like Job, we must take up this wisdom so that we're not mislead by the afflictions brought upon us by satan as to test our faithfulness to God. This is another trick of the enemy; don't fall for it. There is growth in suffering if we walk humbly with our God. He lets these things happen to help us grow stronger, more caring, more loving and more understanding. Suffering can a blessing in disguise. Love those who cause the suffering and pray for them. Jesus our Lord suffered for our sins and we must follow our Lords example to lay down our lives regardless of the cost.

28) Jesus taught us that we should seek the Lord with all our heart, mind, soul and strength so that we would become like Him. Most people would say "That's impossible!" But the Lord would not had told us to be perfect for He is perfect, if it wasn't possible. Again, He said, if it wasn't true, I would have told you. And Jesus alone didn't tell us these things, the twelve apostles and Paul also tell us that the power of Christ is in us. Our job is to believe by faith that these things are

possible by seeking the ways of the Father, seeking His will in every situation we may encounter especially in your marriage. By the grace of God learn to show love, mercy, peace, patience, endurance and grace to your spouse, till death do you part.

DIFFERENT BIBLE TRANSLATIONS

Although I don't like to read, I do however enjoy my meals (spiritual food) and reading is how we eat God's food. I've read and studied my bible over and over and still do. Even still I continue to learn something new every time. I will say, be careful of what you read and believe. Believe the Holy Bible but be careful of other books that do not line up with scripture. I've read many other books. I read only books that will help me with my spiritual journey with my Father and help me with my growth, faith and understanding. However, if it doesn't line up with scripture I may proceed with caution if it has my attention. Once I realize it is misleading, I toss it, and count it as it is, rubbish, good for nothing but the trash can. I strongly recommend that you get a solid understanding of what the bible says to start with, before reading any other book to keep you from being misled. As its written, satan, the father of lies, disguises himself as an angel of light. If you have a firm foundation in the bible, then when you do read something else, you will know if it lines up with scripture or not. If you're not sure, compare it with the scripture, research it, study it, so that you can see if it agrees with the bible or not.

2) I own copies of the lost scriptures (books that the early church has removed) and have read them. I've read these books for my own personal studies, but I don't teach them. I've read the book of Mormon, which I will say I found very interesting and maybe worthy of reading and discussing. However, I do not teach it. I take it into consideration, but I cannot say whether it's true or false. After all, who am I to say what God can or cannot do or will or will not do? Not one single person can say how God will work His will and wonders though out all the earth, throughout all of history, the present age or even in the future.

3) I didn't know at the time that I bought it, but the Bible I'm currently using was and is a Catholic Bible. I found that out while studying. It actually has some extra books and verses that are not in protestant versions of the bible and those books are known as the Apocrypha. For example, the Book of Wisdom, Maccabees 1 and 2 and several others. As far as verses go, I noticed one day while studying the Book of Daniel, that when Shadrach, Meshach and Abednego were on their way to be cast into a fiery furnace that they said a prayer and sang a song, which is not in most other translations or copies.

4) I've also read Old English versions. I have a copy of a pre-1611 King James edition, which I have learned to read. The reason I have this is to better understand the translations. I find it beneficial. For example, in the pre-1611 version the word son is spelled sonne. Our Lords name Jesus is spelled Iesus from the Greek name, which is derived from His Hebrew name Yashuwah.

5) The Jehovah's Witnesses claim that there is only one true name of God and that's Jehovah. The fact is, there are many names for God according to scripture. Although in the old testament God says, "I want you to call me Father". Even Jesus calls on Him as Father and so did the Apostles. I think we should follow Christ example. We should call Him what and who He is, Father.

6) But in this study, we will start by looking at the name Jehovah. That name is a translation from the Greek name Yehouah (notice the v is replaced with a u). Which is translated from Hebrew YHWH (Yahweh). I'm not even sure how it's translated into other languages. In the pre-1611 version there is no letter J but instead it is a Y. Like in the name Joseph its Yoseph. The city of Jerusalem is spelled Yerusalem and Jews are Yews. Even the Vs and Us were not used as they are today in modern English, including our King James copies.

7) What does Jehovah, Yehouah, YHWH even mean? It means I AM that I AM. God told Moses, "tell them that, I AM that I AM, sent you".

What are some other names by which our God goes by? According to scripture His name is Holy, Righteous, Mercy, Glory, Almighty God, Wonderful Counselor, the Alpha and the Omega, at one point God Himself said, "My name is Jealous. God Himself tells us that He wants us to call Him Father. The reason is that He gave us all life and is in fact our Creator. We are His children and He said for us to call Him by what He is. FATHER, ABBA, DAD. Jesus said, unless you become like little children, you cannot enter the kingdom of heaven.

8) The bible is food for the soul, all other books are food for thought. But I will say that our Father isn't done writing books. There are some books besides the bible that can be food for the soul. As scripture says, man shall not live off of bread alone but by the very word of God. By His bread of life, His living waters. Which according to scripture is His Beloved Son Jesus.

9) Another reason to know your bible, is so that you can use it to talk about what God has done and is doing. You don't want to misuse the scriptures and take them out of their original context. Before you quote scripture, pray for wisdom, knowledge and understanding. Pray for the Lord to open your eyes so that you may see, open your ears to hear, for an open and receptive mind and a caring heart. Then, as you listen to the spirit you will know what to say. I've seen churches use the passage from Hebrews 13:16, "For such sacrifices are pleasing to the Lord". To put on their envelopes for the tithes and offerings it receives (And yes, it is good to give your tithes and offerings and its scripture). But what does it say in Hebrews 13: 15-16? It says, Through Him let us continually offer up a sacrifice of praise to God, that is, the fruit of the lips that acknowledge His name. Do not neglect to do good and to share what you have. For such sacrifices the Lord is well pleased. Amen to that.

10) I also enjoy hearing from Jewish Rabbis who believe in Jesus as their Lord and Savior. They usually have a deeper knowledge and

understanding of the original Hebrew scriptures, translations and meaning. In working through all of this I've come to understand scripture a little better. As our Father said, "My word will be spread throughout all the earth. Every tribe, tongue, language and nation will know me." It is true the word of God has spread over the world. It may not always be accepted but it has spread. We should read that word to get to know our Father. We pray to not only begin a relationship with God but to also build a relationship with the Father. Why? Because what God wants is a relationship with us. You see He wants us to love others, more and more, and because as we do so we can love Him more. For it is written, if you cannot love the people around you that you can see, how can you love the one you can't see?

11) Hey, I get it, the Bible is a massive book with thousands of pages. It can be intimidating to even look at. But the more I read it the more I understand it, and the more I understand it, the smaller it gets. Each time I read it; I catch something I didn't catch before. There have been times when I've read something a hundred times and then one day the Lord uses that same passage to reveal a mystery to me. This is another reason we need to read our Bible more than once: There is too much information to get all the understanding in one reading.

12) Now, if you're like me, in my busy season I don't have much time for reading such a big book. The same is true if your a slow reader like me. That's why I can say thanks be to our Father for modern day technology. As the saying goes: they make an app for that. There are many types of bible study apps to help you on your journey. I personally like Bible.is. This is my favorite app by far. It offers a new way of presenting the Bible. In a sense it brings the bible to life. If you have a busy life, I definitely recommend it. You can listen to it through your phone or PC with your headphones while running, working or doing house work. I use it all the time. If you commute to work for an hour one way each day you can go through the whole bible in about 6 weeks. Or if you can listen at work, one can make it through in about 2

weeks. In this way you can familiarize yourself with a lot of scripture in a short amount of time. As you listen repeatedly you will find that you start to memorize parts. I have also found it beneficial to take notes on what you read because it also helps with memory and understanding.

13) I've met many people who say that the King James Bible is the only true version. I would say be extremely careful about this, these people are walking on dangerous ground. What did our Father say? My words will be spread throughout all the earth. To every tribe, tongue, language and nations Including but not limited to old English and all the different modern-day English languages. And not just English, it is to be given to all the languages throughout the earth. If you remember, I mentioned earlier about how the older English versions didn't have the same spelling it does now. How can we expect people to read something they can't understand? It seems that some people just are not happy unless they can stir up arguments. But the scripture says to stay away from meaningless arguments. The King James is a translation from a translation from a translation. I've read and compared many translations and own many different translations. What I have come to find is that they all have the same meaning and concept. Because of that, I have to ask, how is one to preach or teach or receive the message if it's not translated into a language that the reader can understand? All translations are equally important. Can't a person still learn from the word of God and be saved through the word of a modern translation? Yes, he can. All translations of the Holy Scriptures are indeed food for all souls and I count them all as the living word of God and Him as the one true author.

14) God told the Israelites that they should not seek to be like the other nations or follow in their ways, but to follow Him and His ways for His ways are good and lead to righteousness and life. The ways of the world are evil. Now I can't find in scripture where it says that the nations could not or should not follow the way that He told Israel to live. He

has called the people of all nations to follow His ways so that we can all be His children through Jesus Christ.

15) In the Book of Malachi 3:16-18, we read: [16] Then those who feared the Lord spoke to one another, and the Lord gave attention and heard *it*, and a book of remembrance was written before Him for those who fear the Lord and who esteem His name.[17] "They will be Mine," says the Lord of hosts, "on the day that I prepare *My* own possession, and I will spare them as a man spares his own son who serves him." [18] So you will again distinguish between the righteous and the wicked, between one who serves God and one who does not serve Him.

To that I say: Amen, Amen and Amen.

16) I recommend taking notes while reading and on what your hearing from preaching and teaching as well. I would also encourage you to write down your prayers in a prayer journal or even better write a letter to the Father along with your prayers, it is still a prayer even if you write it down. I have one book that is only used for notes taken during church services and for writing down the names of those who need prayer. Create your own book of remembrance. Write down your life's experiences, your walk with God, your testimony, which is never ending. Write about how the Father has worked in your life and what you've done for the Father and your Family. Write down the blessings and the blessed corrections. You will be amazed as to what the Father will show you in doing this.

17) Scripture teaches that if we believe with all of our heart, mind, soul and strength, God, the Father of all creation of whom created all the Heavens and the earth and all that dwell within them will be with us. It teaches us that He sent His only Begotten Son to this wicked world so that anyone that would believe in Him, would be saved. Believe in His teaching, His words, believe in the scriptures that tell us He was beaten nearly to death and nailed to a wooden cross and left for dead. So that He could save a wicked world from their sins. He died for His enemy, He died for His friends. Our Lord, the Son of the Holy Father died for

me, He died for you. So that we all may be called Sons of the Holy Father. We were meant for God. We were meant to be His children, to be brothers and sisters to each other. To be brothers and sisters to His angels and to our Lord Jesus, to love others as Christ loves all of us.

18) Continue to grow according to your calling, to fulfill your calling. Test your armor in the midst of your life. Think of it as on the job training. The more you use it the stronger you will get. Practice your faith and your calling. As our Lord said, according to your faith so shall it be unto you. Practice makes perfect. Practice your faith so you may learn to be perfect in your faith.

19) When our Father put it in my heart to write this book, I remember thinking to myself, what am I going to write? I knew there was a message but what am I wright? I'm no writer. I also remember thinking, well whatever it is, it won't take long. Yet, at the same time I just didn't feel as if I was ready. I was right in thinking that. I would need to pray and study more than ever before. I buckled down and did it and I'm glad I did. Three years after the Father put it in my heart to write this, I finally felt ready enough to get started. Malachi 3:18 lays it all out: "So you will again distinguish between the righteous and the wicked, between one who serves God and one who does not serve Him." Our call is to fear the Father's wrath but love His mercy, His Grace, His children and love His love. He only wants you to come home. Do good, love one another more so you can love Him more.

WORLDLY CHRISTIANS AND THE WORLD

Where should I start? There is much to be said on this subject. The scriptures talk about those who say they are Jews but were not. The same is true for Christians: there are those who say they are Christians and are not. People who say they believe they are saved and that they are going to Heaven but show no evidence of a changed heart; they treat their fellow brothers and sisters like dirt, like scum of the earth. They fuss at them, curse them, steal from them, fight them, sue them, arrest them, lie against them, some will even side with a non-believer against a fellow Christian simply because they are friends or family and maybe even because they are wealthy. There are some in the church who dislike and even hate other parts of the body. They have no mercy or love. Remember what our Father said in the scriptures: they sing praises to My name, but their hearts are far from Me. And also: with their mouth they give honor, glory and praise to My name but with the very same mouth they curse others.

2) If you're a true child of the Living God, then it is important that you do not live in the ways of the world. Just as God told Israel not to live in the ways of the world. Unfortunately, that was their down fall; they wanted to be like the other nations instead of living according to God's ways. They wanted to live in the ways of the world. What did God call Israel? He called them a stiff-necked people, because of the hardness of their heart. It's the same way with the Christian who wants to live in the ways of the world instead of the ways of God. In Luke 16:13-15 and Matthew 6:24, Jesus teaches us, you cannot serve two masters. You will either hate the one and love the other, or you will be devoted to the one and despise the other.

- 3) You cannot serve both God and money. Don't let money come between you and your fellow brothers and sisters. Pay your hired hand what you agreed to pay them, do not hold back, even if you're not happy with the work. If you find they are not meeting your satisfactory, then pay what you owe and send them on their way peacefully. You don't have to bring them back. Find another laborer. But don't send the one you're not happy with empty handed. He has bills to pay and a family to support, just like you. And its scripture. Do you not depend on your income? Would you be happy if the one who pays you short changed you or didn't pay you for the you work had done, simply because they were not happy with your work? How could someone dare say they love God but send their labors home without money to buy food for their families or clothing for their children? I have seen this done by those who claim to be Christians. In fact, I've even had it happen to me. To this very day I have clients who say they are Christians but refuse to pay what I charge. The Lord's earthly brother James writes: "the wages you failed to pay to the workers who you hired to mow your fields, cry out against you. Their cries have reached the ears of the Lord Almighty." Some even boast about how much they make while at the same time saying to the one who does work for them your wages are too high, I'm not going to pay what you ask you'll have to take less. Shouldn't a believer want to see those whom they hire prosper? Our Father tells us in the scriptures, not to send one out empty handed but should pay him what is owed and to pay him daily, for he is poor and depends on the wages to supply for his family.

4) All throughout the scriptures our Father tells us to remember the poor man and help him in any way we are able. There is enough food for all people yet there are people going hungry, why? There are enough homes for every family, yet there are some who are refused homes. In today's world, transportation is a must, yet there are people that are denied the right to drive or own a vehicle. A lot of this is mostly

because of a lack of money or because the government has forced financial burdens on them that they cannot afford. When they can't pay, the government will say, you think you've got it hard now? Wait till I take away your right to drive. Sadly, a lot of these are also Christians. Some people will trash a running car before they will give it away.

5) Many Christians will refuse to sell or rent to another because of their lack of credit or because of their back ground. Even though some of these people are also Christians. There are Christians who will rent to a nonbeliever because he has good credit but deny a fellow brother because of his lack of credit. We see the problem of homelessness, why? Is it because of another's hardness of heart? Jesus taught us in the separation of the goats and the lambs to always consider what the Lord things of us: Are we sheep or are we goats. Do not worldly Christians fall in the category of goats with the unbelievers? He said to the goats: depart from me you workers of evil, for whatever you didn't do for the least of these my brothers, you also didn't do for Me. To the true Christians who are the lambs of God, what did He say? Come into My Father's Glory, for whatever you did for the least of these my Brothers you also did unto Me. Again, remember how He said, the world will know that you belong to Me by how you love one another. Don't do anything against another that would cause them to call out to the Father concerning you in any way. What will you say to the Lord when He ask you about how you treated one of your brothers? God you know that was my job or perhaps one might say I was just following the laws of the land. How do you think those answers will go over at the judgement?

6) Do not let this evil world tell you how you should treat your fellow brothers. Do not sue your brother or take him to the gentile courts but work it out if you are able. Again, some will say "but it is because the laws of the land that I acted this way against my brother." Or they will say but it was because of my job that I had to act this way against my brother. These people have no fear of the Lord nor do they have Christ

abiding in them. These people fear man more then they fear their God. Does scripture not teach us that we should put God's law and rules first, before man's laws and rules? It is written, obey the laws of the land unless it interferes with My laws, and in that case, the Lords law come first. What else does it say? Would you fear man who can only destroy the flesh over Him the Lord who can destroy both the flesh and the soul? Do not mistreat another brother or sister or anyone because it was your job or because it was the law of the land. Do you not know Brothers that to do evil to another is to sin against God?

7) What is the greater sin? to sin against God or man? What do the 10 commandments say: You shall love the Lord your God with all your heart, mind, soul and strength you shall love your neighbor as yourself. We teach our kids that it's a sin if they lie, cheat, steal, bare false witness, covet, commit adultery, kill, worship any graven images or dishonor our parents.
8) What I have not ever heard taught, though it is a commandment is:
It is a sin not to love the Lord your God with all of your heart.
It is a sin not to love the Lord your God with all of your mind.
It is a sin not to love the Lord your God with all of your soul.
It is a sin not to love the Lord your God with all of your strength.
And it is a sin not to love your neighbor as yourself.

9) Worldly Christians are those who say they believe and perhaps they do. Even the demons believe and shutter at the sound of His name. Some Christians, however, do shutter at the sound of His name. They chase after material things. With them a little is not enough. They have to have bigger houses, newer nicer cars, boats, and other stuff. And that still isn't enough, they build houses to store all their stuff while the homeless have no form of shelter except perhaps a cardboard box, a tent, or a bridge.

10) Keep in mind the scripture where Jesus tells the story about the rich man and Lazarus in Luke

16:19-31, [19] "Now there was a rich man, and he habitually dressed in purple and fine linen, joyously living in splendor every day. [20] And a poor man named Lazarus was laid at his gate, covered with sores, [21] and longing to be fed with the *crumbs* which were falling from the rich man's table; besides, even the dogs were coming and licking his sores. [22] Now the poor man died and was carried away by the angels to Abraham's bosom; and the rich man also died and was buried. [23] In Hades he lifted up his eyes, being in torment, and *saw Abraham far away and Lazarus in his bosom. [24] And he cried out and said, 'Father Abraham, have mercy on me, and send Lazarus so that he may dip the tip of his finger in water and cool off my tongue, for I am in agony in this flame.' [25] But Abraham said, 'Child, remember that during your life you received your good things, and likewise Lazarus bad things; but now he is being comforted here, and you are in agony. [26] And besides all this, between us and you there is a great chasm fixed, so that those who wish to come over from here to you will not be able, and *that* none may cross over from there to us.' [27] And he said, 'Then I beg you, father, that you send him to my father's house— [28] for I have five brothers—in order that he may warn them, so that they will not also come to this place of torment.' [29] But Abraham said, 'They have Moses and the Prophets; let them hear them.' [30] But he said, 'No, father Abraham, but if someone goes to them from the dead, they will repent!' [31] But he said to him, 'If they do not listen to Moses and the Prophets, they will not be persuaded even if someone rises from the dead.'".

11) I understand this torment to be the second death, the eternal lake of fire As Jesus put it is a flame that cannot be quenched. This is the Father's eternal wrath and is something to be feared, truly. Oh, that such thoughts would cause people to receive the Spirit of the Fear of the Lord, which is the beginning of Wisdom.

12) What we see from this is the poor are not to be looked down upon but helped. I remind you, because we do not know who is or isn't a child of God. Even if they are not, we should want them to see Christ in us. Paul spoke about worldly Christians. In 1 Corinthians 1:18 and 5:18-19, To those not mature in Christ, he states that they still need

nurturing. Like an infant not ready for solid food but only milk. They need growth. (We have all been at this point and many still are.) Paul said, not to regard them as enemies. He refers to them as brothers and sisters. He knows that some should already be grown up enough to be teachers, but they just aren't ready. They still need someone to teach them again, the basic principles of Christ.

13) I have seen people allowed to teach in churches that were not living what they were teaching. At the same time, I have seen people denied the right to teach who were more than able to do so. Man wants to qualify whom they want instead seeking the one that God has qualified. Man seeks those who have been educated by institutions instead of the one the Lord has schooled by His spirit. We see this especially in the new testament. They asked how Jesus received what He learned when He was not taught by those with earthly authority. Such thinking continued with regard to the disciples. The church would rather have someone who has a letter of recommendation accompanied by a degree than one whom the Lord has taught and called through His Spirit. As the old saying goes, God doesn't call the qualified He qualifies the called. Paul even spoke about those who seek letters of recommendation, instead of recommendations from the heart.

14) We have gone so far that we let the wicked ways of the world tell us how we should run the churches. Forgiveness by God seems to mean little, while a person's past forgiven by God and left in the past still haunts them in the present. What happened to mercy, forgiveness and love? At the same time, I know of churches whose pastors have been to prison for murder. If Paul lived today with his history would we allow him to teach in our churches? Good question. Even in his day, he was kicked out of several churches. Not much has really changed in the world concerning man's heart. Times have changed but the world has remained the same.

15) If God teaches us that we should have mercy and forgive others, then why are we doing background checks to see if one is worthy? Maybe God should do a background check on us to see if we are worthy of His Grace, because I tell you not one person is worthy. Or to see if He will let us in His kingdom! No man is worthy of this either. If a man has repented from his sins and has turned to the Lord, then why do a back-ground check on him? If God has forgiving him then so should you. Would you dare say to a man, it doesn't matter if God has called you to preach or teach; according to your background, you are a sinner and we will not allow it. Are we not all sinners? Again, there seems to be no mercy, forgiveness or love for our brothers. What if a homeless man was in our church every Sunday, would we let him teach a class or preach in a church filled with wealthy people? Probably not.

16) Sad to say but most Christians follow in the ways of the world. They refuse to sell or rent to someone because they have little or bad credit. But to the ones with good credit they will be glad to sell or rent to regardless if they are a believer or not. It seems as if we choose to help the nonbeliever because they have credit but have turned their back on the one who truly needs us. Some Christians will charge interest to their fellow brother. Even worse they will charge recurring interest to their brothers. Interest on top of interest that never stops growing so that it gets to the point that one will owe more in interest then the actual debt owed. We will sell to someone with good credit at a 3% interest while charge one with lesser or bad credit 10% interest. So those with less need are charged less than those with the most need.

17) I've seen Christians take a poor man's belongings because he hit hard times and could no longer pay what he owed. This is God testing our hearts, to see how we're going to handle our power. Will we do it with contempt or love? Do you really love your neighbor as yourself or do you love your money and the ways of the world more? You cannot serve both God and money. Like the rich man who came to Jesus asking, Lord what must I do to inherit the Kingdom of God? Jesus said

to him, love the Lord God with all your heart, mind, soul and strength and love your neighbor as yourself. The man said, all these things I have kept, what do I still lack? The Lord said, if you wish to be perfect, then go and sell all that you have and come and follow me. The man went away in great sorrow because he had great wealth. Then the Lord stated, for this reason it is easier for a camel to go through the eye of a needle then for a rich man to enter the kingdom of heaven. The rich man didn't want to give up the trust and security he had stored up for himself and put his full trust in the Lord. The man didn't love his neighbor as himself, he loved his wealth more than those around him that were in need. That was a test of the heart to see if he would put his trust in God or in his money. He chose to trust in his worldly riches then heavenly riches.

18) God the Father calls us to come to Him, to be His children. Since an atonement must be made for our sins, and no human being is without sin, He sent His only begotten Son to the earth to die for the sins of every single person if they will believe in Him. Jesus prayed, Father, it's not the sacrifice of animals you have desired but sacrifice of the heart. Christ loved the people of the world so much that He not only sacrificed His body but even His heart. So too, we should sacrifice our heart, our all to Him and to believe and follow Him in the same likeness.

19) Look at Paul. Before he became Paul (meaning humble), his name was Saul (meaning asked for). (God asked for him to be humble, or it could be said, Saul to be Paul.). Saul was a Jewish Pharisee, who killed and imprisoned any he found who claimed Jesus as Christ until the Lord humbled him and changed his name to Paul. The plans and calling of the Lord for Paul would change his life in such a radical way, that his whole life was about to be flipped upside down. Paul would spend the rest of his life spreading the very same gospel he tried to destroy. Paul will not only spend the rest of his life teaching it but also suffering for it. He would be shipwrecked, received forty lashes minus one several

times, stoned nearly to death, imprisoned many times, the list goes on. But Paul endured all of this, so the people of the world may hear his eye-witness account and believe in the resurrected Jesus so they could be saved from sin by the amazing grace of the Father.

20) Like a good, good Father, God doesn't reward bad behavior but does reward good behavior. In Psalm 31:19 we read; "no mind can conceive what God has in store for those who love Him. To love Him is to love each other in the same manner." In John 13:34 we read, "a new commandment I give you, that you must love one another, as I love you." (Like the other commandments, if we don't love others as He loves us, then this too is a sin.) Since He loves you, what did He give up so you might be saved? He gave up everything, even His own life. To believe and follow Him to Life and not death.

21) Scripture teaches us that it's not the death of the flesh (the first death) that we should fear but rather it's the eternal death (the second death) we ought to fear. If a wicked man dies in his sin, then he is doomed to the second death. But as we have stated before, God does not delight in the death of a wicked man but that the wicked man shall turn from his wicked ways and do good. If anyone would turn to God with all their heart then the Lord will heal them and they will be saved, they shall surely live and not die. To die as a child of God is to gain life everlasting. We will all die the first death. Most will die the second death (the eternal lake of fire). Some will die and find themselves in life, God's eternal Glory. Because of this we should love the Lord our God, and our brothers and sisters with all our might. Bring others into the Family of God. Run the good race, fight the good fight, love with a godly love, as He has loved us, so we may bring as many as possible to everlasting life and all share together in the harvest into the Father's everlasting Glory.

22) I have always believed that like Israel, our nation was also founded by God through Christian people and developed by Christian

forefather's. We have the words "in God we trust" on our money and in our Pledge of Allegiance it says, "one nation under God." Like Israel we haven't followed God's ways. Instead, we had to do things our own way, following the ways of the world. It says in our constitution that we shall have the freedom of religion. This has been twisted around and used out of context by those who say it means what they want it to mean. Some will say it means that we can worship anything or anyone, anyway as we feel fit. This is not true. Ask anyone who studies historical documents. No Christian leader is going say its ok to worship anything or anyone other than the one true God. If this were true, then they would also be ok with people worshiping the devil. Not even nonbelievers would want this. Nonbelievers would rather have a Christian church in their town than a satanic cult. What the constitution means is that we have the freedom to worship God however we feel free to with regard to differing denominations.

23) Scripture tell us how to worship God, our Father. Praying is an act of worship. Worshiping in the spirit and singing praises is an act of worship. Performing acts of kindness is a form of worship. All acts of love are worship. Giving thanks for all things and situations is an act of worship. Let God's Spirit do the walking and talking praising His holy name and give thanks in all things.

24) About 10 years ago the idea of worship hit me in a whole new way; it was a totally different understanding of what worship was truly about. It will forever change how I feel about worship and how I sing praises. It was a new understanding of how to worship in the spirit. You've probably heard it said that we can learn as much from our children as they will learn from us. It's started with Jesus talking to His disciples about children. He said, unless you become like one of these, you cannot enter the Father's Kingdom. Well, around ten years ago, my family and I were going through a rough patch. For the most part it was because of my errors. During this time my wife and I with our daughter

were at the mall. While we were there, we saw a kiosk where you can record any song and put it on a disc to take home.

24) My daughter really wanted to do this, so we let her. The song she chose to sing was 'Daddy's Hands' by Holly Dunn. To be honest this was the first time I had ever heard the song. As I listened to my 11-year-old daughter sing it to me and for me, it broke me to the core. I couldn't hold my tears in. To this day, it still makes me cry every time I listen it. I use as her ring tone. It's a heart jerker that goes deep into my heart. I could listen to her voice singing that song a million times over and never get tired of it.

25) My point is this, in singing that song to me in a busy mall with no regard for the tons of people that were around she expressed her love for me, her father, without a single care of who would hear her. Expressing her love was all that mattered to her. That love pouring into my ears filled me with love and brought tears of joy to my eyes. If God created love and emotions to be expressed like among human being, how much deeper is His love, His emotion, His weeping for joy over His children when they express their love for Him? Wow, that made me stop and think. That's worship, true worship and that's how we should worship in the spirit....

26) If I love to hear my daughter express her love to me like this (not because I require it, but because she wants to), then how much more does the Father love to hear His children sing to Him. Again, not because He wants to be worshiped but because He desires to hear the love we have for Him as we express it in worship to Him. I've seen people worship many things, people, false gods, animals, cars, the earth, the devil. But God is always saying, "Hey if you want to worship something, then worship me. I'm the creator, I created you, I'm the one who gave you life, I'm the one who provides for you, It is because of Me that you live and have, I AM that I AM, the God, the only God and

besides Me there is no other. I AM your FATHER. Worship no other but Me."

27) Scripture says that God is love, therefore, His love must be greater than our love, His Wisdom, Understanding and council must be greater than our wisdom, understanding and council. Any amount of love or expression of love that we can give is no match for God's love. He is love and He gave us His love to share with others. When you share love, share the love of God that is in you with the world, not in the ways of the world, but in the ways of God, amazing things take place. Again, love the Lord with all of your heart, mind, soul and strength and love your neighbor as yourself. As Jesus said, "I give you another commandment, that you should love one another as I love you". He also said, "All the law and the profits hinge on these two commandments" and "The world will know you belong to me by How you love one another."

28) If you act or speak evil towards another, you have indeed allowed those words to testify against you in such a way as to call out to the Father against you. Scripture says that even if you are all alone where no one can hear you speak, and you speak evil that it will be brought to light and be made known, and that your Father even knows your thoughts and the intentions of your heart. We need to guard our hearts against evil. Guard your heart, mind, mouth, acts, guard your very soul and being. Do not give the enemy anything to use against you. Practice showing and sharing love. In doing this you will learn to grow in love. You will grow to love others more, you will grow to love Jesus more, you will grow to love your Father more, by the spirit that your Father has given you. You will also learn to love the lost more and want to bring them home with God where we find rest; no matter their past, no matter the cost. Seek to find the lost sheep and feed them. Seek the lost so they too may be saved through the blood of Christ, by the Grace of our Father and His love for all of His creation.

29) Get involved with others. Get in church if you're not already. Help in the community, do volunteer work. Cloth and shelter the homeless. Feed the hungry and at the same time pray for them and with them. In doing these things and getting involved it will allow you to grow in some amazing new ways. Not only will you grow but you will experience true joy. Be like your big brother Jesus, As He came to serve, so too we must be servants to each other. In service, we will find true love and true joy. Learn to look through your spiritual eyes and see others for who they truly are: Living souls, your brothers and sisters. If you know they're not in Christ, then know that they are potential brothers and sisters. We need to take caution with regard to the jobs and positions of work we accept. If your job requires that you act in an evil manner towards others, then quit your job and stay far from it. Especially if it causes you to sin against other fellow brothers and sisters.

30) Here are some things I've taken notice of: We leave church and go out to eat. We can almost tell who has been to church by the way they're dressed. Yet we all treat each other as strangers, as sinners. I watch those who say they're Christians, most of them don't even give it a second thought. But there are others like me who watch and pay attention to how Christians treat Christians. In all we do we should be aware that God is watching our behavior as well as Jesus and the angels. But besides that, there are brothers and sisters as well as non-believers watching what you're doing, Some may not be dressed in a way that show they just came from church. You just never know who is watching. Christian cops arrest other believers over foolish man-made laws with no mercy and will even testify against the man in court. The so-called offender may even be found guilty by a Christian judge. Again, with little or no mercy. But these same cops and judges may very well ask God to forgive them of their sins and expect mercy, though they themselves are repeat offenders in relation to God. Still they put others in jail. A poor man goes to jail because he cannot hire a

lawyer for a crime, while a rich man goes home because he can hire a lawyer. They say, the law is the law, but the law is not the same for all. The judge knows the law, right? Why then can two men commit the same crime in the same manner and receive two different sentences? That's not justice. And it reveals that there is no fear of the Lord either.

31) I've seen Christians working jobs and owning businesses that require them to act in a evil manner towards others. To take from one who can no longer pay. I've seen Christian property owners put a man and his family on the street because he lost his job. I've seen Christian property owners say to another Christian, I cannot rent to you and your family because of your credit. I can't hire you because of your credit or other past problems. Christian tow truck driver's repo cars from fellow brothers because he lost his job and is a couple payments behind. I tell you, this is not loving your neighbor as yourself. Scripture says that if you have a problem with a fellow brother, we should take it to the church, not to the gentile courts, yet I have not seen one church act in this way. In fact, I've seen some encourage taking issues to the gentile courts. Christian judges will pass sentence on a fellow Christian and have no problem sleeping well that night having no regard to how he has affected the man. I've seen Christians favor nonbelievers over fellow brothers and sisters for no just cause even when the nonbeliever was in the wrong. These are sinful times indeed.

32) By no means should we allow money, things, or man-made laws come between us. If you are one of those who say "well, he broke the law he deserves to go to jail" then don't you think you should go to hell for sinning against God? Scripture says that no man is without sin and all fall short of the glory of God. Again, scripture says that if you cannot forgive others of their sins how can you expect the Father to forgive you of your sins? We will take a pen from our office job but convict someone to prison for several years for theft. Again, mercy for you but no mercy for others. A policeman will try to keep his own kid out of trouble if they get caught or he might let a friend go but will

convict another person for the same act. As scripture says, they sing praises to me, but their hearts are far from me. And again, with their mouth, they give honor to me but with the same lips they curse others. Always remember scripture says to always let graceful words flow from your lips.

33) Scripture says that we can't take our belongings with us when we die. However, there is something we can take with us. It's people. Scripture says, one plants another waters but God gives the growth. One sows, another reaps but we all partake in the harvest. Keep this in mind.

34) Scripture speaks a lot about angels. In Hebrew 13:1-2 it says, "let brotherly love continue, do not neglect to show hospitality to strangers, for thereby some have entertained angels, unaware." Imagine if there were seven angels appointed to watch over you and you know they're there, but you cannot see them. You also know that wherever you go, they also go with you. Because you're a child of God, they are sent to watch you. How would you live your life? Would you change how you live? Would you change how you treat other people? Would you speak evil words to or about others? Would you still spread gossip about one another?

35) Imagine these angels were carrying a book of remembrance about you, every good and bad word is written in this book. Every good and bad action you do is recorded. What would they be writing about you? According to scripture, this could be possible. Whether or not there are angels watching, God knows all you say and all you do. All that's in your mind and thoughts are known to Him. He knows your heart and scripture says, "man may think that his ways are right, but God weighs the heart". One thing I've learned is you can be in self-denial, you can even lie to yourself, but you cannot lie to your spirit, nor can you lie to God. Therefore, we need to live as if angels are

walking among us because they are. That seems to be what scripture teaches us.

36) In the Old Testament, when Israel was in the desert, Moses told the people that God was walking in the midst of His people. So too is it with us. Not only are His angels walking among us and watching us but so is God, our Father. Our Father is in the midst of us, so we should live as if He hears and sees all that you say and do because He is in your midst.

37) In Matthew 18 we read:

> [23] "For this reason the kingdom of heaven may be compared to a king who wished to settle accounts with his slaves. [24] When he had begun to settle *them*, one who owed him ten thousand talents was brought to him. [25] But since he did not have *the means* to repay, his lord commanded him to be sold, along with his wife and children and all that he had, and repayment to be made. [26] So the slave fell *to the ground* and prostrated himself before him, saying, 'Have patience with me and I will repay you everything' [27] And the lord of that slave felt compassion and released him and forgave him the debt. [28] But that slave went out and found one of his fellow slaves who owed him a hundred denarii; and he seized him and *began* to choke *him*, saying, 'Pay back what you owe.' [29] So his fellow slave fell *to the ground* and *began* to plead with him, saying, 'Have patience with me and I will repay you.' [30] But he was unwilling and went and threw him in prison until he should pay back what was owed. [31] So when his fellow slaves saw what had happened, they were deeply grieved and came and reported to their lord all that had happened. [32] Then summoning him, his lord *said to him, 'You wicked slave, I forgave you all that debt because you pleaded with me. [33] Should you not also have had mercy on your fellow slave, in the same way that I had mercy on you?' [34] And his lord, moved with anger, handed him over to the torturers until he should repay all that was owed him. [35] My heavenly Father will also do the same to you, if each of you does not forgive his brother from your heart."

38) This is another reminder of the importance to love others, even your enemy in the same way the Father loves you. He showed His Mercy by sending His Son to die (nailed to a tree), for His friend and His enemy in order that if we will believe in Him, follow His teachings, love one another and love the Father with all our heart, mind, soul and strength, we may be saved from the eternal punishment and live in the Father's eternal Glory. In this process we are joined to His Holy Family and become a member of His body.

39) Love your brothers and bless them. Help them in any way you are able. Your Father loves a cheerful giver. Do not let the world tell you it's ok to mistreat anyone especially a fellow brother in any way, because it's not, not for any reason. Return evil with good. Do not let man's laws overrule God's laws. Imagine the brothers who go into other countries where it's illegal to teach Jesus, yet they do it anyway, to save souls. No matter what the law says. That applies here as well. Don't let man's laws tell you it's ok to mistreat one another.

40) Jesus said in Mathew 15:6b-9, So for the sake of your tradition, you've made void the word of God. you hypocrites! Indeed, Isaiah was correct when he prophesied about you when he said, this people honors Me with their lips but their hearts are far from Me, in vain do these people worship Me, Teaching as doctrines of men. That means we are to live as the Lord commands and not with regard to man. Again, let me remind you from scripture, don't fear him who can only destroy the flesh, but fear Him who can destroy both flesh and soul. Seek to have the Spirit of the fear of the Lord. This is the start of Wisdom. As it says in Isaiah 11:3, concerning Jesus, "His delight will be in the Fear of the Lord." Follow Jesus example.

CHRIST AND THE DIFFERENT DENOMINATIONS

I have one very important question: Should our Lord's church be divided? Absolutely not! But it is, and I ask, why? It's because of selfishness that the church is divided. All because someone doesn't agree with another person or doesn't like what is being done to the church building. If you ask me, like Israel, I believe every church building should be called a Temple of the Lord or A House of Prayer. But, as it is, there is division amongst His children. As scripture says, what you meant for evil I will use for My good. This verse is true in so many different ways. If you truly open your eyes, there is so much evil out there. Scripture says these are indeed evil times, but our Father knows how to take evil and turn it to good for His children. I see it happening all the time now. I think with the different denominations, He will use division, (even though it is a bad thing,) to do good. There are strong, true believers in all denominations, there are also weak believers in all denominations. These weak believers have to learn to turn their whole heart to God. They are living in the ways of the world.

2) If you are part of a denomination that says their way is the only way to heaven then get out of there now, this is a lie, do not fall for this trap. The church existed long before that denomination existed, and the church will continue forever. Do not be close minded and hard hearted by limiting the work of God to just one denomination. The weak still need growth. They are not ready for solid food; they still need milk.

3) The truth is we are all the body of Christ. We are all God's children. However, just like the Israelites, we often want it our way. Perhaps we say things like: tell us sweet things (like so many rulers in scripture said to the prophets). We often don't want to hear God's word unless it is

sweet to our ears. We would rather settle for a lie of sweet words than the truth about our own evil works.

4) Fighting and arguing over things that don't matter is a real problem. A good example of the division of God's children looks like in scripture is when Israel, Judah, were always fighting each other. God repeatedly reminded them to remember they were a family, to stop fighting each other.

5) Jesus sees all of our conflicts and quarreling over matters that are meaningless and worldly. Why can't we remember that we are family? We are all children of the Living God. The new testament tells us that we are the body of Christ. If you are in Christ then you are a part of the body. If that's true then I would encourage you to grow into what God has called you to be. Learn what your job is and go to work. The more you use your gifts to do your job the more experience you will gain, the stronger you will become, and soon, doing your job will become second nature to you.

6) As time goes by you will find yourself doing more work for your Father than for man. Not only that, but you will find that God will give you the opportunity to minister to others even while you are working your day job. It happens to me all the time. Over time I've come to realize the importance of putting my Father's business first. We all should be about our father's business and when God opens an opportunity to minister you should jump on it.

7) We find in 1 Corinthians a division starting to come up in the church. Paul quickly tried to warn them of this in chapter 1:

> [11] For it has been reported to me by Chloe's people that there is quarreling among you, my brothers. [12] What I mean is that each one of you says, "I follow Paul," or "I follow Apollos," or "I follow Cephas," or "I follow Christ." [13] Is Christ divided? Was Paul crucified for you? Or were you baptized in the name of Paul?

8) It's the same kind of stuff that has led to all the different denominations. Some are Baptist, some are Pentecostal, some are Catholic and so on. Did any of these denominations die for you? Were you baptized in the name of your denomination? No, you were baptized in the name of Christ, and Christ died for you. It's okay to give a name to identify the different individual places of worship but it's not right to divide the church of Jesus into rival factions.

9) We should live for Christ, in unity. In 1 Corinthians 3, I find need to repeat the whole chapter:

> And I, brethren, could not speak to you as to spiritual men, but as to men of flesh, as to infants in Christ. [2] I gave you milk to drink, not solid food; for you were not yet able *to receive it.* Indeed, even now you are not yet able, [3] for you are still fleshly. For since there is jealousy and strife among you, are you not fleshly, and are you not walking like mere men? [4] For when one says, "I am of Paul," and another, "I am of Apollos," are you not *mere* men?
>
> [5] What then is Apollos? And what is Paul? Servants through whom you believed, even as the Lord gave *opportunity* to each one. [6] I planted, Apollos watered, but God was causing the growth. [7] So then neither the one who plants nor the one who waters is anything, but God who causes the growth. [8] Now he who plants and he who waters are one; but each will receive his own reward according to his own labor. [9] For we are God's fellow workers; you are God's field, God's building.
>
> [10] According to the grace of God which was given to me, like a wise master builder I laid a foundation, and another is building on it. But each man must be careful how he builds on it. [11] For no man can lay a foundation other than the one which is laid, which is Jesus Christ. [12] Now if any man builds on the foundation with gold, silver, precious stones, wood, hay, straw, [13] each man's work will become evident; for the day will show it because it is *to be* revealed with fire, and the fire itself will test the quality of each man's work. [14] If any man's work which he has built on it remains, he will receive a

reward. [15] If any man's work is burned up, he will suffer loss; but he himself will be saved, yet so as through fire.

[16] Do you not know that you are a temple of God and *that* the Spirit of God dwells in you? [17] If any man destroys the temple of God, God will destroy him, for the temple of God is holy, and that is what you are.

[18] Let no man deceive himself. If any man among you thinks that he is wise in this age, he must become foolish, so that he may become wise. [19] For the wisdom of this world is foolishness before God. For it is written, "*He is* THE ONE WHO CATCHES THE WISE IN THEIR CRAFTINESS"; [20] and again, "THE LORD KNOWS THE REASONINGS of the wise, THAT THEY ARE USELESS." [21] So then let no one boast in men. For all things belong to you, [22] whether Paul or Apollos or Cephas or the world or life or death or things present or things to come; all things belong to you, [23] and you belong to Christ; and Christ belongs to God.

10) Now I am a member of a church that is affiliated with General Baptist, but I simply claim to belong to the body of Christ. We belong to Christ; Christ belongs to God and what belongs to Christ is God's. I follow Christ not a denomination, this what my Father and His Spirit teaches us in His word. The more I grow, the more that the Father teaches me and the more I share with others and the more that I grow. In other words, the more I love, the more I grow, and the more I grow the more I love that process will continue to repeat itself for the rest of my life.

11) In many cases differing denominations come into being because people in a congregation couldn't agree with one another. They wouldn't or couldn't be one in the spirit of God and so they separated themselves from one another. The body of Christ was torn in two so that someone could satisfy their own way of worship and then take others with them. This is a form of division brought on by greed, selfishness, and disbelief, and it is evil. Now as scripture tells us, what

man meant for evil (division) God will use in some way to support His body.

12) We should not allow theologies and theories to divide us because division hinders the growth of the body and the advance of God's kingdom. We should be focusing on what is important striving in the power of the Holy Spirit to be in agreement, and unified by The Holy Bible. If you believe something outside of scripture, keep it to yourself, do not condemn another because they believe something different. Just stick to scripture and prayer to our Father for understanding. Again, I ask, should our Lord's church be divided? The answer is no. Instead the body of Christ should be united in the Holy Spirit. We are called and commanded to be unified and in agreement. Jesus said "they know not the scriptures nor the way of the Kingdom." Concerning the Pharisees and priests Jesus said: "Listen to what they have to say for they know the scriptures well enough but don't be like them, don't follow in their ways." This is another reason to know the scriptures fully, it will help keep you from being misled.

13) There have always been pastors and priests who favor the rich and are harsh to the poor. Those type of people mislead their brothers and sisters because they are still of the world, by using their pastoral authority to take advantage of and abuse members of their congregation for their own selfish ways. May God change their hearts. But until He does, we must guard our heart, soul, mind, and mouth from the evil that tries to hinder us from being all that we can be in Christ. We must learn to guard our entire self from those who will not teach the whole truth found in God's word. Sadly, this is still an issue in many churches. Be careful of the church you choose, test it to see if it holds up to scripture. If it doesn't measure up to scripture, then go somewhere else. If it's in your power, speak up and let it be known how the scripture is being abused.

14) I want to remind you that for all its flaws, church is important. In many ways, the church is like your family at home. We are happy when we gather together, regardless of whose house we gather at. We get together, tell stories, eat and enjoy the fellowship. It should be much the same at church. We should be like a bunch of siblings gathering at the Father's house, to fellowship and build relationships with each other. I myself, enjoy visiting other churches and meeting other fellow brothers and sisters because in a true since, my brothers and sisters in Christ all are like long lost brothers and sisters I have not yet met. When we do meet, it is with much joy and pleasure. I often wonder how many feel the same way because you certainly can't tell by the way some people act.

15) In the various churches I've attended and even my regular church I've found that some people just don't like some people. Sometimes when I greet people they don't greet me back and in fact some are down right rude; not just to me but to others both inside and outside the church. That can't be a good thing. I've heard people say that only the wealthy are worthy of God; the poor are poor because they are worthless to God. I once had someone tell me that I wasn't worthy because I was just a poor hired laborer. If I had been a new believer at the time and didn't know better, such hypocrisy could have pushed me away. Thanks be to our Father, I knew better. Shame on them and anyone who thinks like that.

16) Some people have introduced themselves to me by letting me know that they were children of God. Yet after just a few minutes of getting to know them it became apparent that they were racists and didn't like certain people regardless of whether they were believers or not. Such people are not building God's Kingdom but tearing it down. Divisions, divisions, divisions. I don't like those kinds of people. I try to not allow my heart to be hardened by their ways of being. I would rather that we come together in love and peace.

17) I have times met people who say they are Christians but when I call them brother, they are quick to reject me because I'm not a part of their fellowship. These people's hearts are hardened to the truth because they're still living in the world. The truth is if you're a Christian and you say to another Christian, I'm not your brother, then God isn't your Father and Christ isn't your Lord. Much of this kind of stuff comes from people who don't know the scriptures or they interpret the scriptures in a way that limits who can be in the body of Christ. I've seen many people who wear a cross around their neck and act or speak evil to others. This breaks my heart because such people have no what it means to be a Christian. This is heart breaking, not just to the one being mistreated, but even to the one bringing on the evil, because they have no idea of the judgement, that they are bringing upon themselves.

18) When you hear someone preaching or teaching, don't just take their word at face value but check what they are saying with the scriptures to make sure they are speaking in accordance to the scriptures. We should always be on guard and do not allow ourselves to be misled. We must continually keep our eyes on Christ. Jesus tells us to pay attention to how people are treated in the church. How are the rich are treated versus the poor? We must watch what people do and what they say so that we can discern the hearts of those we fellowship with.

19) As it is written in James 2:

> My brethren, do not hold your faith in our glorious Lord Jesus Christ with *an attitude of* personal favoritism. [2] For if a man comes into your assembly with a gold ring and dressed in fine clothes, and there also comes in a poor man in dirty clothes, [3] and you pay special attention to the one who is wearing the fine clothes, and say, "You sit here in a good place," and you say to the poor man, "You stand over there, or sit down by my footstool," [4] have you not made distinctions among yourselves, and become judges with evil motives? [5] Listen, my beloved brethren: did not God choose the poor of this world *to be* rich in faith and heirs of

the kingdom which He promised to those who love Him? [6] But you have dishonored the poor man. Is it not the rich who oppress you and personally drag you into court? [7] Do they not blaspheme the His Holy name by which you have been called?

[8] If, however, you are fulfilling the royal law according to the Scripture, "You shall love your neighbor as yourself," you are doing well. [9] But if you show partiality, you are committing sin *and* are convicted by the law as transgressors. [10] For whoever keeps the whole law and yet stumbles in one *point*, he has become guilty of all. [11] For He who said, "Do not commit adultery," also said, "Do not commit murder." Now if you do not commit adultery, but do commit murder, you have become a transgressor of the law. [12] So speak and so act as those who are to be judged by *the* law of liberty. [13] For judgment *will be* merciless to one who has shown no mercy; mercy triumphs over judgment.

[14] What use is it, my brethren, if someone says he has faith but he has no works? Can that faith save him? [15] If a brother or sister is without clothing and in need of daily food, [16] and one of you says to them, "Go in peace, be warmed and be filled," and yet you do not give them what is necessary for *their* body, what use is that? [17] Even so faith, if it has no works, is dead, *being* by itself.

20) Here's a homework assignment; read chapter 4 and 5 of the book of James, more good points on this subject. Hope this helps some of you to get into your bible.

21) I've spoken with some Christians who ask me what denomination I'm a part of. As always I tell them I'm a member of a church that is First General Baptist affiliated but I don't claim to belong to any denomination. I am simply a member of the Family of God. They often reply just stay with the Baptist. Isn't this what we just read about with regards to making distinctions amongst ourselves? Why do so many choose to remain blind to these truths? I certainly know brothers and

sisters from other denominations who I believe may have far more growth and maybe even have a better relationship with the Father than I do. Should they be denied salvation through Jesus Christ by the grace of the Father simply because they are members of a different denomination? Of course not. God is clear: "I will have compassion on whom I choose to have compassion and I will show mercy to whom I choose to show mercy."

22) If you believe that your denomination is the only way, then let this be a warning to you. Get out of your closeminded ideas, and cast satan out of your head. Such lies come from the father of lies who seeks to destroy God's kingdom and take you down with him. Open your heart to receive God's true love, His true understanding and share that with others. We are all called to be a part of God's Family. We are called to be His children and therefore, to be brothers and sisters to one another. To do this requires love. Not just any love will do either but a godly love, brotherly love, the kind of love that is merciful and forgiving, a kind of love that is sacrificial. A Holy Love.

23) The bible teaches us that we all have different gifts and that we are all the body of Christ. The gifts that you have been given are meant to go from you to every believer. Every believer is uniquely a part of the body of Christ. And each of us has a job to do. Remember when Jesus was 12 years old, and where His parents found Him after being separated from them for several days? They found Him at the Temple. What was His response to them? He said, didn't you know that I should be about My Father's Business? So too must we be about our Father's business. Dress for work every morning by putting on your Armor of God (and carry our cross daily as Jesus said). Every day we need to put on our armor and, learn how to use it then test it and grow into it. Be imitators of our Lord, King, our Brother Jesus, as scripture teaches us to be. As you live each day seek to discover and use your gifts and use them to serve others, in love, from your heart.

24) Too often we allow small things to divide us as a people, as a church. Many will set their own set of rules, by laws and beliefs out of their own stubbornness and greed and say to others, "If you believe like we do, you can be a member. If not, you can still come but you can't really be a part. Being rejected like that by fellow brothers and sisters because we may believe in something a little different hurts deep. If that ever happens to you, don't be alarmed for yourself but be alarmed for the church.

25) If you believe in the scriptures and you are seeking to live as they tell you too then know that you are accepted by the Father. You don't need to believe in man-made bylaws and beliefs to be a member of God's Holy Family. Christ died for all of us. Always remember, all men fall short of the Glory of God the Father. Man's ways are not God's ways and God's ways are not man's. With that said, if you know you are living a sinful life, then acknowledge it, confess it, repent and turn from your wicked ways and turn to the Father with all of your heart and do good and your Heavenly Father who loves you will heal you and bless you.

26) I long for there to be unity among us all. We are called by God to be in unity, in one accord, all on the same page. Whatever the issue, good or bad, let us all be in agreement. Be in peace with one another. Don't allow worldly issues to come between you and your brother. I've seen people leave their church over the stupidest things like paint color or what kind of carpet to get. Don't be like this. Handle these things with love not hate.

27) We are called to not return evil with evil but return evil with good. Vengeance is not ours to take, so don't seek it. Our Father is clear, "vengeance is Mine, thus saith the Lord". We do as our Lord commanded. Our call is to show mercy. As we read earlier, mercy rules over judgment. For in showing mercy and doing good to someone who has done evil, in love, you just might help save their soul. If this

happens vengeance isn't needed. If they don't come to repentance then the Lord will deal with them. That's not our job. We do as the Lord commanded us, His children: love one another, show compassion and mercy, forgive and give.

28) Imagine the awesome godly power the church would have if we were all in one accord. If all the churches could set aside their differences and focus on the big picture instead of their own little piece of the puzzle. Oh that we would come together in what is important: Jesus Christ and His words and teachings. As He told us, call no man on earth teacher for you have only one teacher, The Christ. Love one another with a pure heart. How much more could we accomplish if we did this? It's no wonder we have a hard time pulling people in, they don't know where to go. They just see a kingdom full of bickering and fighting against one another. The result is we lose even the ones we have because of our hardness of heart. If our churches worked the way Paul taught the churches to live like Christ, I can only imagine the difference it would make. I read recently that a study was done and it was found that most people leave the church for lack of Christ like love. So, some churches started coming up with ideas to get people back in. None of the ideas I read included showing Christ love, which was the problem.

29) Should we as God's children sit back and turn a blind eye to all these matters that are tearing His kingdom apart? Are we going to sit back and let satan try to tear down our Father's House? I love my GOD, my Father. I love my Lord Jesus, my Brother, and I love you who are reading this too much to sit back and watch my fellow brothers and sisters dig their own grave because they aren't being fed and therefore can't grow. (This is one of the many reasons I believe the Lord has put it in my heart to write all of this down. It is my prayer that those who read this will have their eyes open and begin to truly see, their ears opened so they can hear, and their heart and mind opened so that they

may perceive truly. (Hey, I'm included in this too. I pray that I learn from what I've written as much as you).

30) What can we all agree on? God is the Father. That Jesus Christ is the Son of God. Jesus is Lord. He was born of a virgin woman by the Holy Spirit of God. He was sent by God (as all the prophets). That He died on the cross for our sins (as God's perfect lamb, the perfect sacrifice). That He arose three days later and then ascended to the Father. As Christians we should all agree on those things.

31) Yet, believing in Jesus and being saved is not enough we also need to act. As we read earlier in James chapter 1:

> [14] But each one is tempted when he is carried away and enticed by his own lust. [15] Then when lust has conceived, it gives birth to sin; and when sin is accomplished, it brings forth death. [16] Do not be deceived, my beloved brethren. [17] Every good thing given and every perfect gift is from above, coming down from the Father of lights, with whom there is no variation or shifting shadow... [22] But prove yourselves doers of the word, and not merely hearers who delude themselves. [23] For if anyone is a hearer of the word and not a doer, he is like a man who looks at his natural face in a mirror; [24] for *once* he has looked at himself and gone away, he has immediately forgotten what kind of person he was. [25] But one who looks intently at the perfect law, the *law* of liberty, and abides by it, not having become a forgetful hearer but an effectual doer, this man will be blessed in what he does.

32) The goal is to be like Jesus, to follow Him, to follow hHim is to listen to Him and obey. God the father spoke from heaven saying: This is My beloved Son, in Whom I AM well pleased, listen to Him". I want to add to that by saying Jesus is our beloved Brother, who does the will of the Father and in His doing, the Father is well pleased, listen to Him. That is what we should be doing. It's completely ok to have different beliefs in the small things. These small beliefs are only a matter of opinion (according to scripture) and they are not worthy of arguing

over. To do so is a form of selfishness and is evil against your brother and sister. Paul addresses this in Romans 14:1-23:

> As for the one who is weak in faith, welcome him, but not to quarrel over opinions. [2] One person believes he may eat anything, while the weak person eats only vegetables. [3] Let not the one who eats despise the one who abstains, and let not the one who abstains pass judgment on the one who eats, for God has welcomed him. [4] Who are you to pass judgment on the servant of another? It is before his own master that he stands or falls. And he will be upheld, for the Lord is able to make him stand.
>
> [5] One person esteems one day as better than another, while another esteems all days alike. Each one should be fully convinced in his own mind. [6] The one who observes the day, observes it in honor of the Lord. The one who eats, eats in honor of the Lord, since he gives thanks to God, while the one who abstains, abstains in honor of the Lord and gives thanks to God. [7] For none of us lives to himself, and none of us dies to himself. [8] For if we live, we live to the Lord, and if we die, we die to the Lord. So then, whether we live or whether we die, we are the Lord's. [9] For to this end Christ died and lived again, that He might be Lord both of the dead and of the living.
>
> [10] Why do you pass judgment on your brother? Or you, why do you despise your brother? For we will all stand before the judgment seat of God; [11] for it is written, "As I live, says the Lord, every knee shall bow to me, and every tongue shall confess to God." [12] So then each of us will give an account of himself to God. [13] Therefore let us not pass judgment on one another any longer, but rather decide never to put a stumbling block or hindrance in the way of a brother. [14] I know and am persuaded in the Lord Jesus that nothing is unclean in itself, but it is unclean for anyone who thinks it unclean. [15] For if your brother is grieved by what you eat, you are no longer walking in love. By what you eat, do not destroy the one for whom Christ died. [16] So do not let what you regard as good be spoken of as evil. [17] For the kingdom of God is not a matter of eating and drinking but of righteousness and peace and joy in

the Holy Spirit. [18] Whoever thus serves Christ is acceptable to God and approved by men. [19] So then let us pursue what makes for peace and for mutual upbuilding.

[20] Do not, for the sake of food, destroy the work of God. Everything is indeed clean, but it is wrong for anyone to make another stumble by what he eats. [21] It is good not to eat meat or drink wine or do anything that causes your brother to stumble. [22] The faith that you have, keep between yourself and God. Blessed is the one who has no reason to pass judgment on himself for what he approves. [23] But whoever has doubts is condemned if he eats, because the eating is not from faith. For whatever does not proceed from faith is sin.

It continues to say in chapter 15:1-13,

"We who are strong have an obligation to bear with the failings of the weak, and not to please ourselves. [2] Let each of us please his neighbor for his good, to build him up. [3] For Christ did not please himself, but as it is written, "The reproaches of those who reproached you fell on me."[4] For whatever was written in former days was written for our instruction, that through endurance and through the encouragement of the Scriptures we might have hope. [5] May the God of endurance and encouragement grant you to live in such harmony with one another, in accord with Christ Jesus, [6] that together you may with one voice glorify the God and Father of our Lord Jesus Christ. [7] Therefore welcome one another as Christ has welcomed you, for the glory of God.

[8] For I tell you that Christ became a servant to the circumcised to show God's truthfulness, in order to confirm the promises given to the patriarchs, [9] and in order that the Gentiles might glorify God for his mercy. As it is written, "Therefore I will praise you among the Gentiles, and sing to your name." [10] And again it is said, "Rejoice, O Gentiles, with his people." [11] And again, "Praise the Lord, all you Gentiles, and let all the peoples extol him." [12] And again Isaiah says, "The root of Jesse will come, even he who arises to rule the Gentiles; in him will the Gentiles hope." [13] May the God of hope fill you with all joy and peace in believing, so that by the power of the Holy Spirit you may abound in hope."

33) I have seen with my own eyes and heard with my own ears, of churches charging for food and drink before and or after service. I have seen little children turned down and sent away because they didn't have enough money to buy what was being offered. What do you think Jesus would have said if He were standing there? I tell you, He was and is standing there. He is in that child that was just turned away. Should we dare deny a child food or drink that is being served especially in our Father's House? No! We should not and it needs to stop now. As our Lord stated, "My House shall be called a House of Prayer, but you have turned it into a den of thieves." Also, what did Paul have to say about this kind of act? Let's see, in 1 Corinthians 11:17-34 it reads as follows:

> [17] But in the following instructions I do not commend you, because when you come together it is not for the better but for the worse. [18] For, in the first place, when you come together as a church, I hear that there are divisions among you. And I believe it in part, [19] for there must be factions among you in order that those who are genuine among you may be recognized. [20] When you come together, it is not the Lord's supper that you eat. [21] For in eating, each one goes ahead with his own meal. One goes hungry, another gets drunk. [22] What! Do you not have houses to eat and drink in? Or do you despise the church of God and humiliate those who have nothing? What shall I say to you? Shall I commend you in this? No, I will not. [23] For I received from the Lord what I also delivered to you, that the Lord Jesus on the night when he was betrayed took bread, [24] and when he had given thanks, he broke it, and said, "This is my body, which is for you. Do this in remembrance of me."

34) I say this, if you're eating in public (or anywhere you're eating) and someone is near you hungry, then feed him. In doing so, your also feeding Christ. Remember, whatever you did for the least of these my brothers you also did for Me, says the Lord. Especially if you're in

church (a House of Prayer) you shall not charge for food or drink. It would be better not to serve food or drink at all if you're going to charge. Regardless, you should not eat or drink around others who are too poor to buy for themselves, unless you're willing to pay for them to eat.

35) I was visiting with an old friend one day and he told me they stopped going to church because of the way they were treated. I asked what happened, and he informed me that they charged a membership fee. When this family could not afford to make their fee payment the church revoked their membership. They could still attend but they could no longer be a member. What happened to the love and mercy that we are supposed to have for the poor that come to our door? This is not how God, Jesus, Paul, or the scripture teach us to treat the poor. Is this church charging people to be a member of God's Family? Woe to those who do this. I once had a client, a couple counties away, tell me their church had taken them to court and was having their checks garnished for not paying their tithes and membership fees.

36) In Ezekiel 34, God sends Ezekiel out to deliver a message to the priests (the shepherds). The priests weren't doing their job! Although they were working as priests, they were not doing what God had called and instructed them to do. They had stopped acting by His command. God said to those priests: "With force and harshness have you ruled My people". Sadly, this still carries on today. This passage talks about God's children (the sheep) not being tended to but actually being led astray by the priests (shepherds) and His sheep being thrown to the wolves (the world) to be devoured by the wild beast (satan).

37) The priests did not care about the people. They started to get greedy and demand that the people give more, more than God had commanded them. They had no concern for the people, for their brothers and sisters. Nor did they have any fear of the Lord. They were so calloused toward God that they turned against God's command on how to perform the

sacrifice, out of greed abusing their authority and power and thereby robbing their brothers and sisters of their grace and blessing and at the same time destroying the relationship between God and His people.

38) Think about this for a minute. Do we have sons and daughters, family members or friends whom we love, who do not believe? Don't we do what we can to help them and provide for them? Shouldn't we be all the more concerned for those who do believe? After all they are our true brothers and sisters. Do not neglect the poor believers, because they too are our brothers and theirs is the kingdom of heaven. And whoever belongs to Christ is called to be one with Him, that means Christ is one with us as He is with the Father. So, if we mistreat someone in the body of Christ it is the same as if we mistreat Jesus. On the other hand, to show love, mercy and to do good to someone, is indeed showing love, mercy and doing good to Christ. And we ought to do this because Christ first loved us, showed us mercy and did good for us.

39) As these writings come to an end. I pray that this book will help you in your walk with God our Father and in your relationship with Christ Jesus, our Lord, our King, our brother. As well as, help you truly learn what it means to love your neighbors, your brothers and sisters in Christ, your enemies and those that persecute you. May God give you the grace to grow stronger and stronger in the Lord and to grow weaker in the things of this world.

40) I pray that our Father will truly open your eyes, ears, heart and mind to truly know how He expects His children to live with and show love for one another. Let His will be done on earth as it is in Heaven. The kingdom is near you, in you and all around you. Live here now as if you are already in Heaven. May you learn to truly love the Lord your God with all of your heart, mind, soul and strength. This is the first commandment and the second is like the first: You shall love your neighbor as yourself.

41) I will continue to pray that you dress for work. Don your armor. Go out into the world (but don't be of the world). Imitate your Lord Jesus, and be like Him, be about your Father's business. Grow your Father's business by bringing in more people as you learn to love on them. May we truly show the world that we belong to Him by HOW we love one another. May our Father's Peace and Grace be with us all.   AMEN

42) Jesus Prayer for All Believers from John 17:

When Jesus had spoken these words, He lifted up His eyes to heaven, and said, "Father, the hour has come; glorify your Son that the Son may glorify you, [2] since you have given Him authority over all flesh, to give eternal life to all whom you have given Him. [3] And this is eternal life, that they know you, the only true God, and Jesus Christ whom you have sent. [4] I glorified you on earth, having accomplished the work that you gave me to do. [5] And now, Father, glorify me in your own presence with the glory that I had with you before the world existed. [6] "I have manifested your name to the people whom you gave me out of the world. Yours they were, and you gave them to me, and they have kept your word. [7] Now they know that everything that you have given me is from you. [8] For I have given them the words that you gave me, and they have received them and have come to know in truth that I came from you; and they have believed that you sent me. [9] I am praying for them. I am not praying for the world but for those whom you have given me, for they are yours. [10] All mine are yours, and yours are mine, and I am glorified in them. [11] And I am no longer in the world, but they are in the world, and I am coming to you. Holy Father, keep them in your name, which you have given me, that they may be one, even as we are one. [12] While I was with them, I kept them in your name, which you have given me. I have guarded them, and not one of them has been lost except the son of destruction, that the Scripture might be fulfilled. [13] But now I am coming to you, and these things I speak in the world, that they may have my joy fulfilled in themselves. [14] I have given them your word, and the world has hated them because they are not of the world, just as I am not of the world. [15] I do not ask that you take them out of the world, but that you keep them from the evil one. [16] They are not of the world, just as I am not of the world. [17] Sanctify them in the truth; your word is truth. [18] As you sent me into the world, so I have sent them into the world. [19] And for their sake I consecrate myself, that they also may be sanctified in truth. [20] "I do not ask for these only, but also for those who will believe in me through their word, [21] that they may all be one, just as you, Father, are in me, and I in you, that they also may be in us, so that the world may believe that you have sent me. ²² The glory that you have given me I have given to them, that they may be one even as we are one, ²³ I in them and you in me, that they may become perfectly one, so that the world may know that you sent me and loved them even as you loved me. ²⁴ Father, I desire that they also, whom you have given me, may be with me where I am, to see my glory that you have given me because you loved me before the foundation of the world. ²⁵ O righteous Father, even though the world does not know you, I know you, and these know that you have sent me. ²⁶ I made known to them your name, and I will continue to make it known, that the love with which you have loved me may be in them, and I in them."

The sinner's prayer

If you're new to the faith and would like to be a part of this

Holy Family that God the Father is calling you to join, then all you need to do to start your journey to life everlasting, into His everlasting Joy, Grace, Peace and Love. Then you can start by praying this simple prayer:

God, my Father, Blessed be your name.

Father I know that I am a sinner,

and I have sinned against you and your Kingdom.

I ask you for your mercy and forgiveness.

I believe that the Christ, Jesus is your Son, who you have sent.

I also believe that He died for my sins,

and that you raised Him to life everlasting.

I want to trust Him as my Savior

and follow Him as my Lord, from this day forward.

To guide my life and to help me to do your will

I pray this in the name of your Son Jesus,

Amen.

Notes

Notes

Book of Remembrance

Malachi 3:16

Names of those you know and meet who fear the Lord

April M Stewart ♡

Joshua D Lassiter - So Proud of you!

Hunter Clark - keep it up

I Sign your Book

you Sign Mine

Made in the USA
Columbia, SC
21 July 2019